ILLUSTRATING ARCHAEOLOGICAL ARTIFACTS

ILLUSTRATING ARCHAEOLOGICAL ARTIFACTS

Volume I

Janie Ravenhurst

Library of Congress Control Number: 2022920065
ISBN: Hardcover   978-1-6698-5286-5
                 Softcover   978-1-6698-5287-2
                 eBook   978-1-6698-5285-8

Print information available on the last page.

Rev. date: 10/27/2022

To order additional copies of this book, contact:
Xlibris
844-714-8691
www.Xlibris.com
Orders@Xlibris.com
532626

CONTENTS

INTRODUCTION

Directors of archaeological projects are always seeking people who can illustrate the artifacts that they uncover. Often, any one of us who is capable of drawing is given the task to draw artifacts, even though we may not know exactly how to go about it. We try looking for instruction online, or in libraries, getting advice from others, but find very little. Eventually, we manage to find a way to illustrate through trial and error. Often the illustrator is also asked to train undergrad students in the basics of artifact illustration, thus necessitating the availability of a hands-on guide, with numerous illustrations, to give any novice the basics of the skills needed and a text to refer to.Hence, the seed of inspiration for this simple, step-by-step publication, Illustration of Archaeological Artifacts was planted.

This publication is unique in that it describes, pictorially, how to draw artifacts. The emphasis is on the use of illustrations rather than words. In Volume I, the reader will learn about: The Tools of the Trade (Chapter 1); how to illustrate pottery and ceramic vessels (Chapter 2); and how to illustrate lithics (stone tools) (Chapter 3). In Volume II, the reader will learn how to draw 3-dimensional artifacts made from various materials such as clay, stone, glass, bone, metal, and fabric (Chapter 1); how to recreate and bring the past to life with reconstruction drawings of artifacts, people using artifacts and how to recreate realistic architectural environments (Chapter 2); and finally, the reader will learn about the value of technology in illustrating artifacts: how to use cameras, computers, scanners, photocopiers and the WACOM tablet to create, record and archive drawings, as well as ink and prepare illustrations for publication (Chapter 3)

Although this publication is not an exhaustive description of illustration techniques dealing with all possible issues, it does offer a strong base for the beginner to build on. With continued drawing practice, skills are perfected. Experience is what gives an artist a quick and accurate hand which can never be taught in one easy lesson but is learned over time. All it requires is a willingness to start, and determination to continue.

Attempting the feat of illustrating artifacts can sometimes be frustrating. Being artistic certainly helps but is not a requirement. If you are dexterous enough to write your name, you have all the ability in your hands that you require. Artist's hands are no different than anyone else's. All that's needed is proper equipment, patience, and a good eye for detail.

Good luck to all of you!

CHAPTER 1

Tools of the Trade

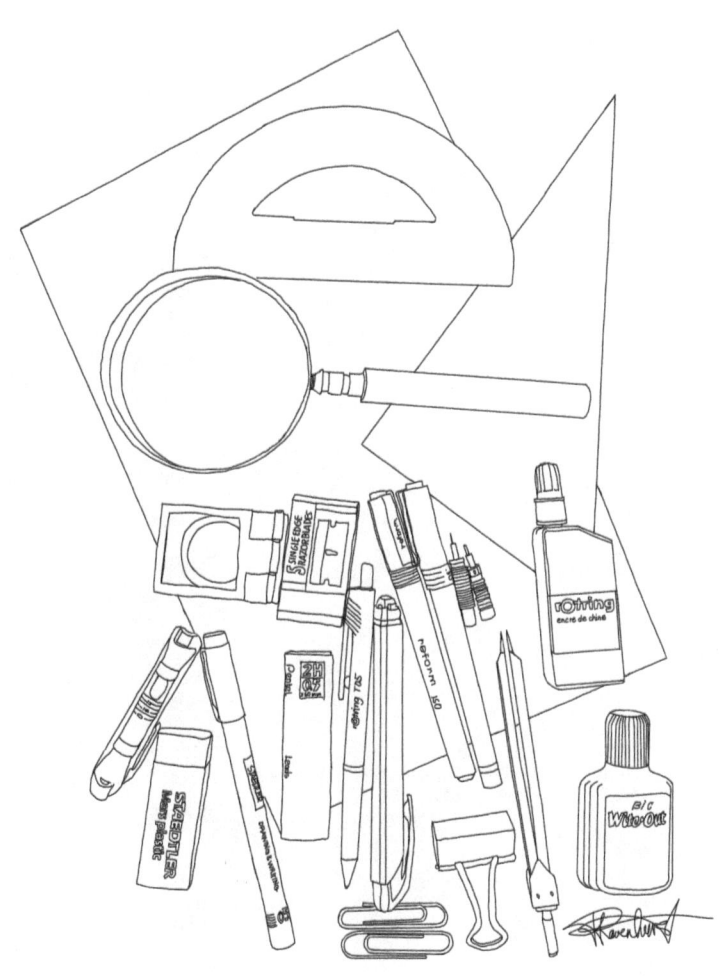

CHAPTER 1

Tools Of The Trade

When you work in the field as an illustrator, you begin to realize the value of having the proper 'tools of the trade'. Although it is always best to keep things as simple as possible, it is of paramount importance that these tools are of the best quality possible. For this reason, it is suggested that illustrators bring along all their own tools. That is the only way you can be assured that the quality of the tools will not make your work more difficult, nor slow you down.

a) Necessities

Light: The most important factor in illustration is light. Without the proper light, details are missed, and progress is very slow. That's frustrating for you and the archaeologists you are illustrating for. If possible, find a location outside, under a portico so you benefit from the light but not direct sun. If there are no outside porticos, then a desk in front of a bright window is the next best thing. Make sure the light falls on the left-hand side of the artifact and the shadow is on the right as this is the usual convention used when we illustrate artifacts and try to capture their 3-D quality.

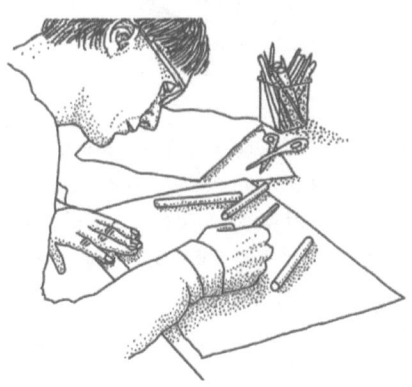

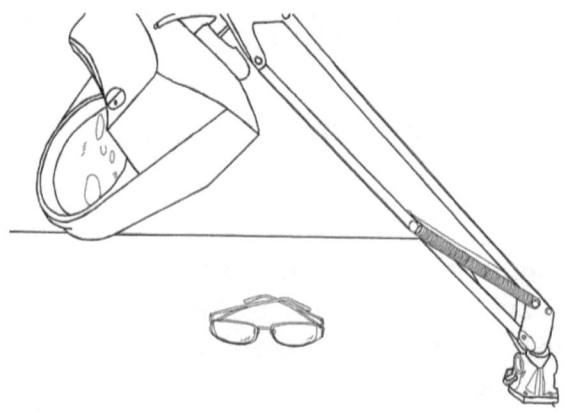

<u>Vision</u>: Being able to see high detail each day, all day long, is of paramount importance. Make sure you have the best glasses necessary. Also, bring along magnifying glasses and Optivisors which give you hands-free magnification and reduce eye strain.

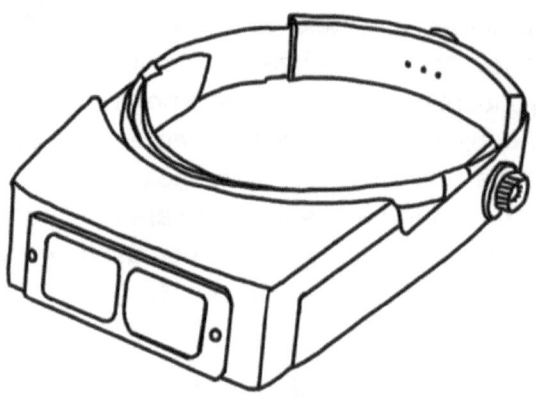

<u>Paper:</u> is the next most important item. It is very important to have good quality paper, otherwise all your work could be for nothing. Always bring your own paper with you. This may seem excessive; however, spending time searching for paper when you are already at the archaeological project can be a frustrating waste of time. There are many great brands of paper available in cities in Canada, the USA, Europe, Asia and Australia, but not usually in remote areas where the excavations occur.

The different stages in the illustration process require different kinds of paper. For the initial drawing, I prefer a thin but strong see-through paper that will not tear easily and will hold pencil lead without smudging. I usually use Canson Tracing Calque 11x14 25lb or Borden and Riley #41 Parchment Tracing 11x14 25lb papers. Vellum can also be used. These brands have all sorts of paper types and sizes that come in a convenient pad form: easy to travel with and easy to keep organized. I tape or paperclip this thin paper to a sheet of graph paper and then draw on that. The grid is visible through the vellum so I can be sure that the various drawing views of an artifact are positioned correctly on the page, are in line with each other and are not skewed. Remember to add a 5cm scale to each page. Also remember to write down the artifact numbers, the date, page # and your name on every sheet of drawings.

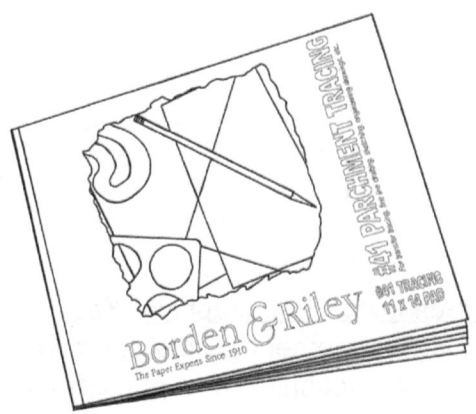

If you are inking on paper, the best paper to get is mylar. This is strong, see-through paper that the ink doesn't bleed into and doesn't warp when the ink is put on it. This can be expensive; however, it is worth it. Trying to ink on cheap paper that the ink bleeds into and doesn't allow errors to be corrected, can be very frustrating. Place the mylar over the drawing and graph paper and then ink. Remember add the 5cm scale to the inking. Also, remember to label the inkings with artifact #, page 3, your name and date.

Archiving Drawings/Inkings. It is very important to keep the drawings and inkings organized and protected/archived. Place tracing paper between drawings and inkings and place in a zippered portfolio. If an excavation area is particularly dusty, place the illustrations in a plastic bag in the portfolio for extra protection. Also, to avoid smudging and for easy viewing put all the drawings in an Itoya's Art Portfolio which is a portfolio with clear plastic pages. 11x14 or 14 x17. These come in all sorts of sizes, and will keep the drawings from fading, yellowing and smudging. This is a wonderful way to display your work and protect it at the same time.

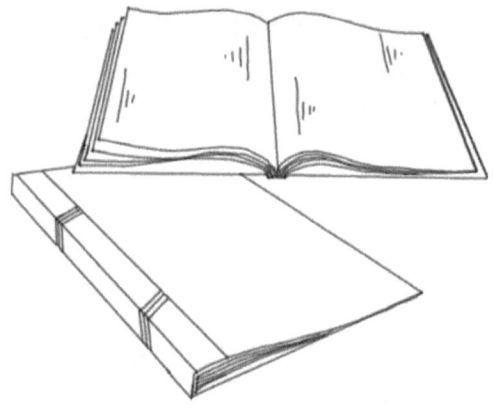

Record Keeping/Scanning/Photographing: Keeping a record of all your work in various places other than just one portfolio is important. This can be done with scanning and photographing and saving the information in pdf or tiff files. Scanning is more accurate than photographing your drawings. The bigger the flatbed scanner, the better. That way you can have all the views of an artifact in one file. When you scan the drawings or inkings, make sure you have a small black and white scale 5 cm long in the scanning as well. That way the size of the image can be changed from 1:1 without losing awareness of the actual size. The scans can be used for ease of viewing and sending to various archaeologists and publishers. The quality of the drawing scans can be less than 1200 DPI as those will be used easily on the WACOM tablet for inking but won't be published. Scans of the inkings will need to be at 1200 dpi or more for the best quality publication. Label, number, and group all the scans of the drawings and inkings in appropriate files. Photographs of drawings and inkings are not as accurate as scans. The value of the photo depends on whether the camera is held perfectly level or not. If not then the photo no more than an inaccurate pictural record, but better than no record at all.

WACOM Tablet: The WACOM tablet might not be considered a necessity, but it does make the inking and archiving process much easier. Using the WACOM tablet with Photoshop may initially be expensive but the benefits are outstanding and well worth the investment. The tablet can speed up the inking process, is much less messy than traditional inking (errors are fixed quickly) and can prevent issues concerning finding and purchasing the best paper. Also, copies of drawings and inkings are easily stored and can be sent quickly via the internet as pdf, tiff or psd files.

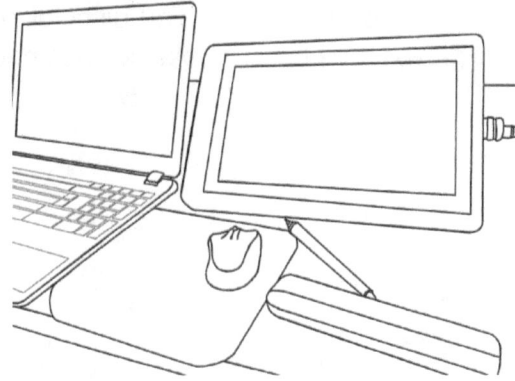

TOOLS OF THE TRADE

b) Measuring, Drawing and Inking Tools – The Basics

- Fabric Gloves
- Pencils
- Erasers: white, kneadable erasers, stick erasers
- Plastic rulers
- Clear plastic triangle/set square with measurements marked along the sides
- Protractor

- Line level and string
- Plumb bob and string
- Compass, dividers
- Plastic calipers
- Molding profile gauge
- Pens, ink, nib cleaning solution, cotton swabs
- Magnifying glass/reducing glass
- Razor blades
- Exacto knives/Scissors
- White out
- Clear tape, paper clips
- Music
- Snacks/ Water

Fabric Gloves: Whenever possible, wear gloves when handling artifacts. That way the oils and dirt from your hands do not become embedded in the fabric of the objects and discolor or disintegrate the object. Fabric gloves are best. The plastic ones become hot and uncomfortable.

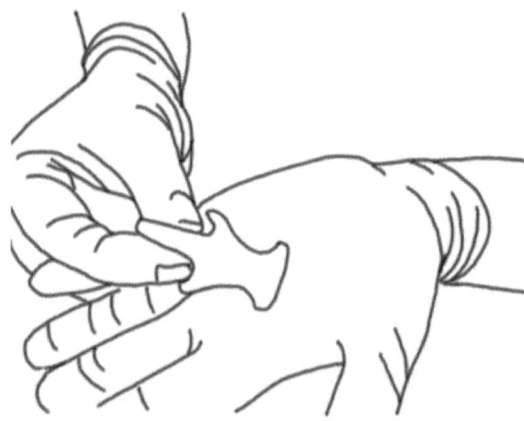

Pencils: Pencils can make or break a drawing. Too soft, and the illustration smudges. Too hard and the paper might rip, and the lines could end up too light and difficult to see. I tend to use either an H or 2H mechanical pencil for my drawings. Mechanical Pencils are very time-efficient to use and don't require stopping work to sharpen them. Make sure you bring extra packs of pencil lead refills. These pencils create drawings that don't smudge, and all the details remain clearly visible on the paper long enough to scan them and put them in a portfolio for protection.

Erasers: are also very important when drawing. I often have the big soft white erasers which also serve as platforms for the artifacts. They can also be cut into various shapes to support an artifact. The kneaded erasers are also very useful for the same reason. However, for correcting errors in my drawings, I mostly use the white erasers in a pencil-shaped eraser holder. These are the most convenient and work the best.

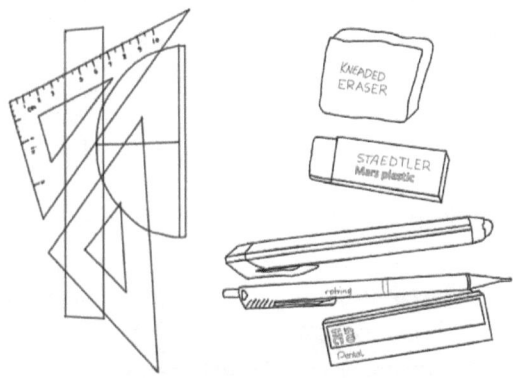

Ruler, triangle, set square, protractor: With all these measuring tools, it is best that they are made of plastic, not metal. Metal can damage the artifact and plastic is soft and see through. It is very important to have clear numbers marked along the edges and right up to the corners. If the numbers are faded, then accurate measurements cannot be done. If the numbers don't go all the way to the bottom or side edge of the set square or triangle then again, accurate measurements cannot be achieved. Staedtler products have measurements to the corners of the triangles.

Line Level and string: These can help when trying to find the horizonal base line for an artifact. It is also useful when triangulating lithic flake scars or seeing how horizontal the base or rim of a vessel is. Also useful for profile mapping on site.

Plumb bob and string: This can help when trying to find the vertical center line of an artifact or the depth of the inside of a complete vessel. Also, very useful for surveying and mapping unit profiles on site.

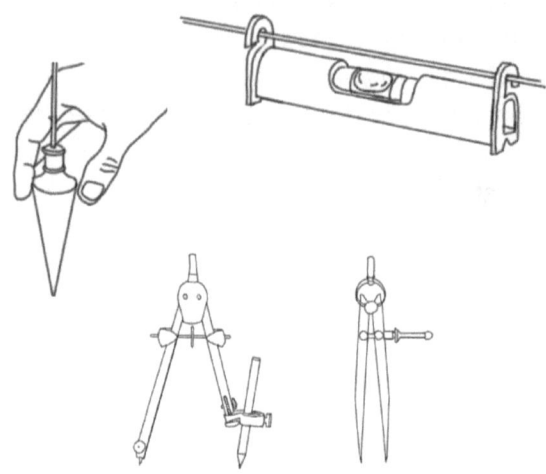

Compass and dividers: are very valuable, having a few uses when drawing artifacts. The compass with pencil or pen holder can be used to make the diameter ring chart, draw top or bottom views of vessels, and recapture the circular paint designs on pottery. They can also be used to measure distances between points and to triangulate a flake scar point on a lithic artifact. Dividers look like a compass but don't have the pencil or pen holder. They are used to triangulate or measure the distance between two points.

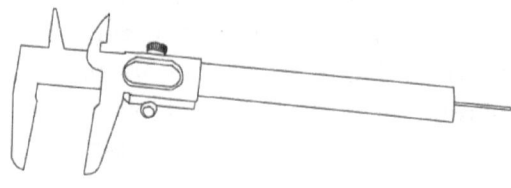

Calipers: As with the plastic measuring tools, it is best to use plastic calipers or at least calipers with plastic on the inside of the measuring arms. This is so that the artifact won't be damaged by the metal. The calipers are used much like the dividers to measure the distance between two points and then transfer that measurement to paper.

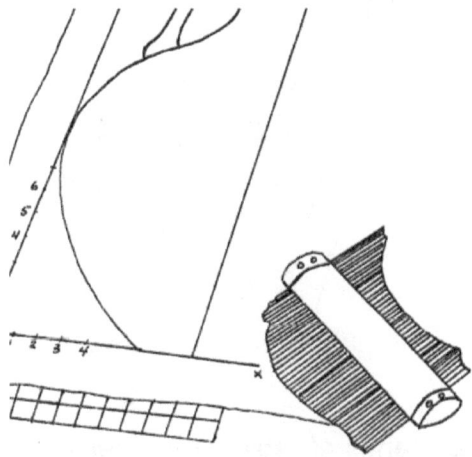

Molding Profile Gauge: This tool is used to measure the profile of the molding in houses. However, it is very convenient when measuring profiles of archaeological artifacts as well. I cannot suggest using plastic profile gauges, because they don't work as well as the metal ones. So, when using the metal gauge, great care must be taken to not damage the artifact by pushing the gauge in to the artifact. Instead, hold the gauge up to the artifact and then push the tines towards the artifact until they touch it. The resulting profile can then be transferred to the drawing on the paper.

Pens and Ink: Once all the views of the artifact are drawn the illustrations need to be inked. I never ink over the pencil drawings. Not only can the lead block up the nibs of the pens, but the original work is forever lost. It is much wiser to keep the pencil drawing on file in case the inked illustration gets lost.

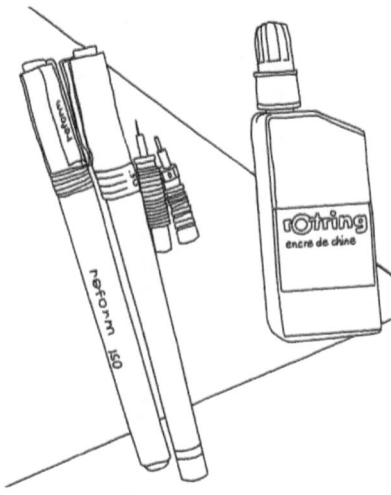

There are several brands of rapidograph pens available in stores: Staedler, Kohinor, Rotring are 3 examples with internal ink reservoirs. The nibs are not interchangeable between the brands, so experiment before purchasing too many. You can buy one body and 3 interchangeable nibs in one brand to try them out. Generally, you need only 3-5 nib sizes. These sizes are numbered differently with each brand: 0-4 Staedler, 00, 0, 1, 2, 3 Kohinor. Anything smaller usually plugs up very quickly and is frustrating to work with.

Always use the correct type of ink for specific nibs. Each brand has their own ink. Make sure to bring enough with you so you don't run out. Ink not specifically for rapidograph pens will clog the nibs. Make sure you bring cleaning supplies for the pen nibs, including a washing liquid and q-tip swabs. Pen nibs need to be kept moist. They can be put in water at the end of each day to prevent clogging. Sometimes the nibs become so clogged they need to be taken completely apart and cleaned but great care must be taken to not to bend the stylus inside the nib casing.

Because most inked drawings are reduced in size for publication, it is best not to go too fine with your pen nib, as the lines will disappear/ blend together in the publication. There is nothing worse than seeing your beautiful illustrations reduced to a blobby mess when published. Using the reduction glass can help you to see if the line width in your inking is too small and needs to be thickened before reproduction and publication. A quick reduction photocopy can also work.

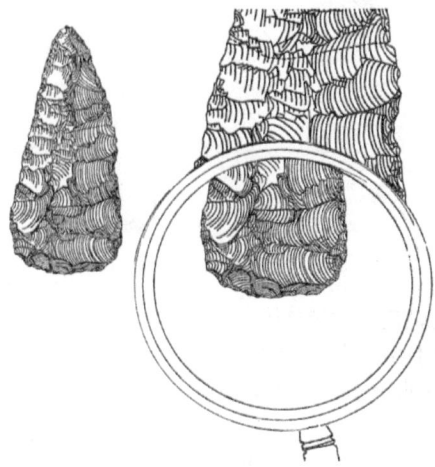

Reduction Glass: A reduction glass is very valuable for checking to see if your inking has its lines or dots too close together and cause blobbing in publication.

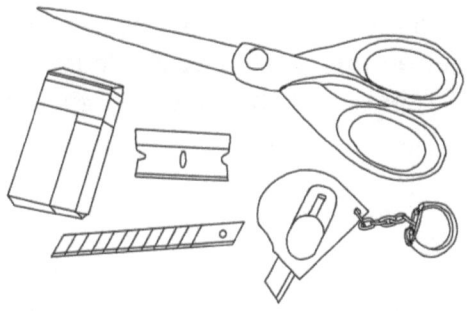

Exacto knives/Backed razor blades/scissors: The exacto knives and backed razor blades are very handy for cutting small 5cm scales and scratching away errors in ink on mylar. No white out needed! Scissors, of course for cutting mylar, tape, string etc.

Whiteout: to fix errors in an inking if not on mylar and if you don't have exacto knives.

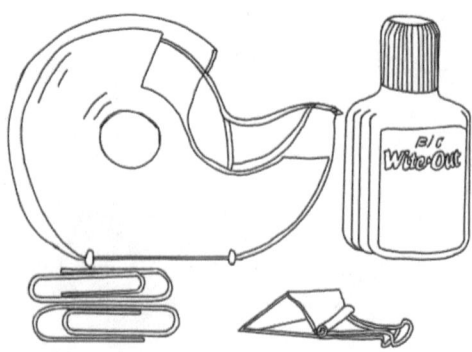

Clear tape/paper clips: Used to hold the drawing paper securely onto the graph paper, hold the mylar for inking onto the drawing paper, and organize drawings in batches.

They can also be used to hold protective paper over the drawings or inkings.

Music: This may seem unimportant. However, when trying to keep yourself sitting in the same chair for many hours, drawing, without getting bored, music is the best remedy. Books on tape, online courses, and recorded seminars are also very good for this. Don't forget to get up and stretch every hour if you can or if you remember. A short session of chair yoga will avoid stiff muscles and re-energize you!

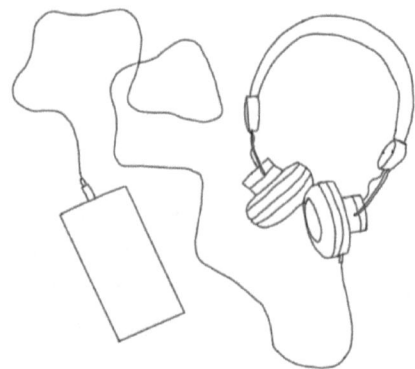

<u>Snacks and Water:</u> These are also very important to have if you are going to be sitting in one spot for an entire day. Food and water for body and brain will avoid falling asleep, getting grouchy, or making too many mistakes in your drawings.

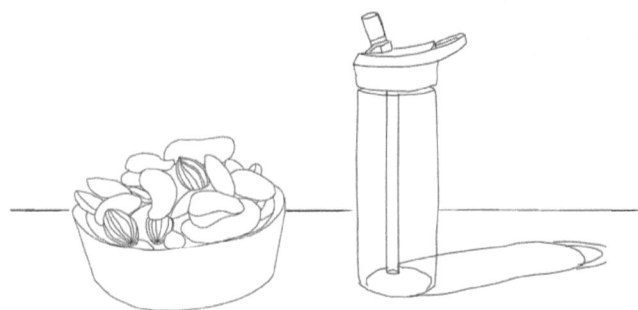

<u>Keep Detailed Records</u>: Finally, keep a record of all your illustrations. As mentioned, make scans of all drawings and inkings. Number, date and sign all the pages of illustrations. Create a spread sheet list of all the illustrations. An excel spreadsheet database is the best way: Artifact number, description, date, portfolio page number, pencil drawing, ink drawing, photograph, scan, notes. Keep multiple copies of these lists on a portable hard drive, thumb drive, personal computer, project computer, project database. Then there is very little chance of information loss in the future. Just make sure that if anything is corrected or changed on one file, that it is changed on all the copies of the file to avoid confusion.

Now that you have the supplies you need, and you know how to protect and archive your work, you are ready to.......

....start drawing!

CHAPTER 2

Ceramics/Pottery

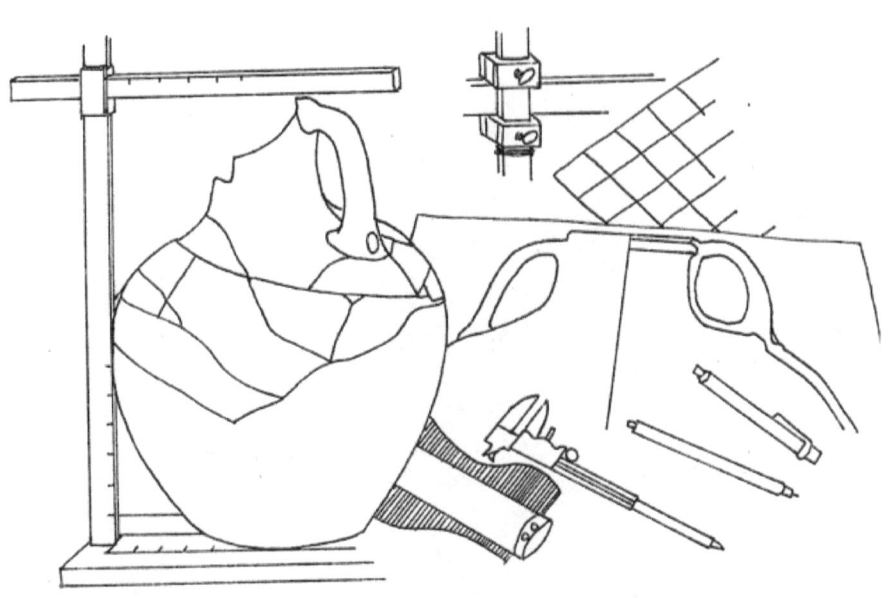

CHAPTER 2

Ceramics/Pottery

Pottery is part of the ceramics category of artifacts. Ceramics refers to artifacts, made from clay, cement or glass, and are usually the most abundant artifacts found on sites dating after the aceramic neolithic period. Ceramic artifacts include pottery (bowls, plates, cups) as well as floor and wall tiles, bricks, roofing materials and sculptures both large and small. Even glass objects are considered ceramic. On many sites, pottery is the most abundant ceramic artifact found, so we will focus on pottery in this chapter.

Usually only pieces, or sherds of pottery, and occasionally whole vessels are found. Valuable information can be gleaned from sherds, such as the thickness of the vessel walls, the vessel profile, and the original stance of the vessel. This is assuming, for simplicity's sake, that the vessel was evenly produced all around like a perfect wheel-thrown pot which hadn't sagged before firing and didn't have any other blemishes.

If an entire vessel is found, it will be important to capture any asymmetry in the lip, base, neck, or body which can't usually be captured from single sherds. Then similar techniques to those used when drawing 3-dimensional objects can be used.

In this chapter we will be covering how to draw rim, base and body sherds as well as entire vessels.

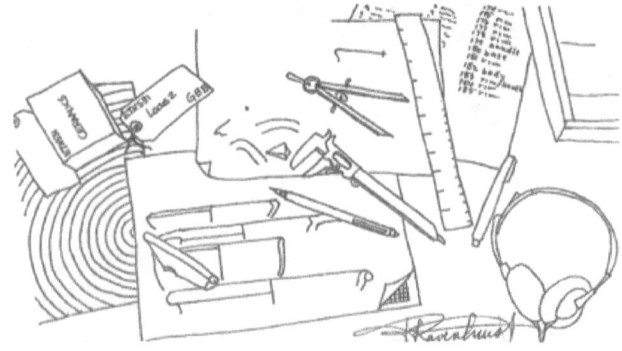

CERAMICS/POTTERY

a) Rim Sherds

Some wheel-made vessels were dried upside down on a flat surface before firing in a kiln or oven. Therefore, the top of the rim can be flat. When we find rim sherds, and we place them upside down on a flat surface, so that the top of the rim is flat, we can see how the original vessel used to look, albeit upside down. This technique of placing the rim sherd upside down on a flat surface helps us to reconstruct the original position, or stance of the vessel. Of course, this is based on this assumption that the rim is contiguously flat on top, which may not apply to all vessels. However, with only sherds to work with we make some assumptions that make our drawings more a rendition of what the vessel may have looked like.

To prepare for drawing a rim sherd, first get all your supplies together: drawing vellum and tracing paper, calipers, graph paper, pencil, eraser, ruler, clear triangle, diameter ring chart (see below), and mould measuring gauge. Place a sheet of vellum over a sheet of graph paper to start.

Then, find the stance of the rim sherd. Do this by placing the top of the rim on a flat surface. Check whether the top of the rim is totally flat by looking to see any light is passing between the top of the rim and the flat surface on which it has been placed. You can also rock the upside-down rim back and forth until you can see or feel the entire surface of the top of the rim being flat on the surface. Hold the sherd there.

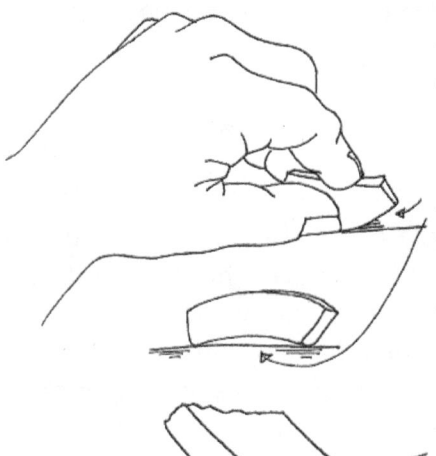

If light passes through between the rim top and the table either in the middle or at the sides, then the stance is not correct.

Adjust the stance until the rim is totally flush with the table until no light passes through underneath the top of the rim sherd. Now the stance is correct

Use this stance to find the inner and outer diameter of the rim. Place the rim upside down in the correct stance position, on a diameter ring chart.

Hold the rim at the correct stance and move it long from one diameter ring to the next, until the curve of the rim matches that of the drawn ring. Both the interior and exterior curve of the vessel can be measured, although the interior is initially more valuable as you will see in the next steps.

(Create your own diameter ring chart by drawing full or partial circles with a compass on a piece of paper. The circles should be 1-2 cm apart. If possible, after drawing all the rings, cover the paper with clear plastic to avoid rips, tears, and discoloration)

Next, use a ruler to draw a horizontal line at the top of your drawing paper. In the example above, the exterior of the rim is 8 cm wide. Measure and mark 8 cm on straight line which you drew on your paper. At the center of this line, drop a vertical line approximately the same length as the height of the rim sherd.

Measure the thickness of the rim and place a mark on the horizontal line indicating this.

Note: If the rim has a larger diameter than your paper, change the horizontal

I line with a wiggly line in the middle and write down what the true diameter is. When the illustration is inked, it will have to be drawn with the true diameter, making the inking larger than the original pencil illustration. This method will help to keep the original pencil illustrations at a manageable size. It can also save time, especially when time is at a premium in the field. This will not compromise detail or accuracy in any way.

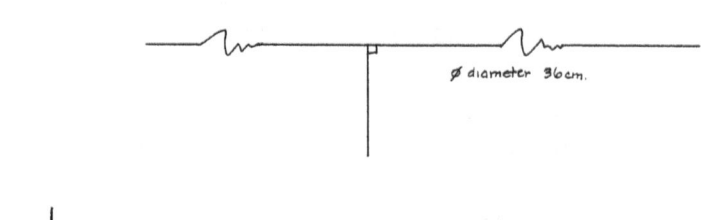

∅ diameter 36cm.

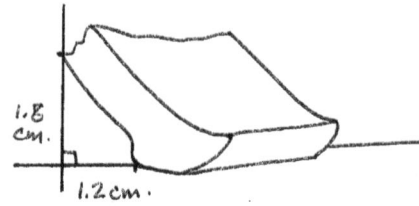

Next, take the sherd off the diameter chart and put it on any piece of paper. You will be gathering stance information to accurately transfer that to the paper. Hold the sherd at the correct stance on this scrap paper. Put a mark on the interior of the sherd where it touches the paper. Next, find the angle of the stance by measuring out from the sherd where it touches the table, and measure up from the table to the highest interior point (see diagram) You can use a clear plastic right angle triangle here and mark on the paper, where the corner of the triangle touches the paper. If the triangle has rulers marked on both sides of the triangle this can be very helpful at this point.

Measure and transfer the horizontal and vertical measurements to the good copy paper. Measure horizontally from the center line and vertically down from the horizontal line on the right side of the drawing. (North American method)

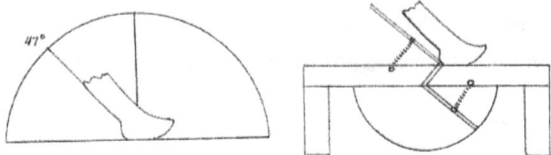

Note: If you are uncertain if the stance is correct or not, indicate it as an estimate.

Some illustrators use a protractor to aid in determining the stance of a rim.

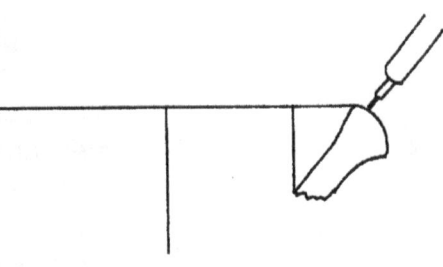

A rimometer, using a protractor, is an interesting invention that could help with the difficulty of correctly finding the stance of a particularly challenging rim sherd

Once the horizontal and vertical measurements have been placed on the paper, the precise cross section of the profile can be drawn. This can be done in several ways. The simplest way is to set the sherd on edge, close one eye, and trace around the sherd.

However, this is not always the best way, as care must be taken to avoid leaving a lead residue on the artifact. This technique also results in a slightly thicker cross-section than reality. Therefore, the rough outline can be traced carefully in and then thicknesses must be verified with calipers.

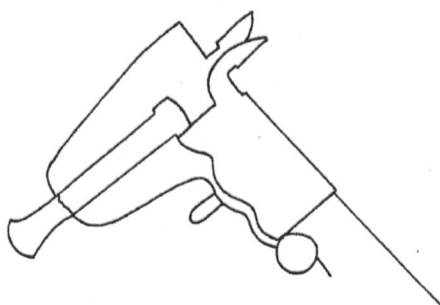

As a quick side note here, it is important to mention that some publications present their vessel drawings with the cross section on the right and the exterior profile on the left. This is mostly the North American way. Others, usually from Europe, reverse this.

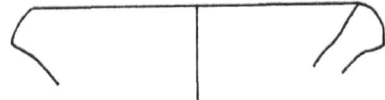

Make sure to ask the project director, which format you will be expected to use.

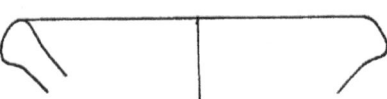

An alternative method is to use a gauge.

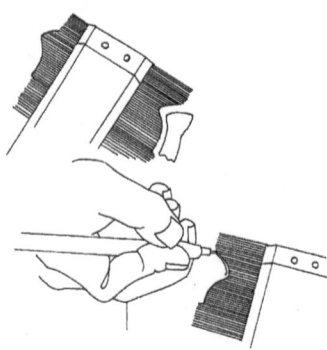

Most moulding profile gauges are used to measure wall trim. However, they can also be very helpful when illustrating artifacts. They are either made from metal or plastic. The metal ones are more accurate, but there is one caveat. Do not press the artifact **into** the gauge or vice versa. This will damage the artifact. A safer way is to hold the artifact up to the gauge wires on one side and then carefully, push the wires from the other side up against the object. When you have an accurate profile shape, take the gauge away from the object, keep the profile shape intact, and place it flat on the paper. Line it up in the correct position with the horizontal and vertical baselines. Trace the outline/profile.

The interior profile of the sherd can be drawn in the same way.

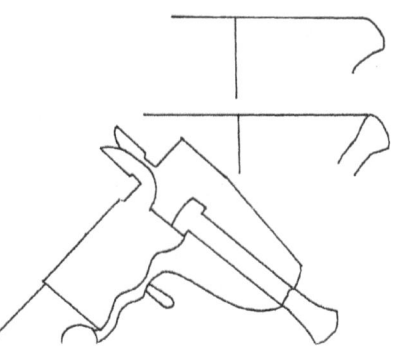

Compare the thicknesses of the sherd with those in the drawing with calipers and correct where necessary.

With the cross-section completed and drawn on the righthand side of the baselines, you now need to draw the profile of the sherd to the left of the vertical line. The best way to achieve a perfect mirror image of the right side is by tracing.

Put the tracing paper over the drawing. Mark a small cross at the intersection of the horizontal and vertical baselines. Now trace the profile.

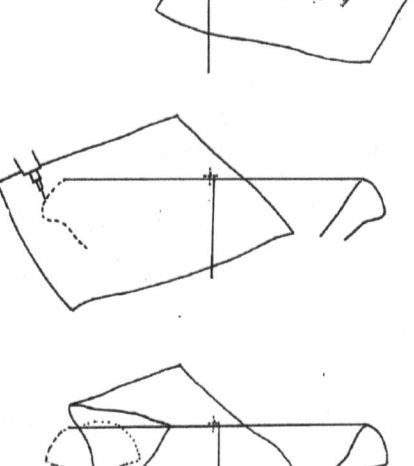

Flip the paper over facedown and line up the small cross at the intersection of the horizontal and vertical baselines. Also, line up the end of the horizontal baseline with the top of the traced rim sherd profile. Trace the profile from this back side of the paper, pressing hard enough that the lead on the back of the paper will come off onto the paper underneath.

Take the tracing paper away and darken up the very light rim sherd outline underneath. You don't need to trace the interior of the sherd profile on this side.

Now your rim sherd profile is complete.

At this point you can add in any exterior decorations on the left half of the drawing and any interior decorations on the right half of the drawing.

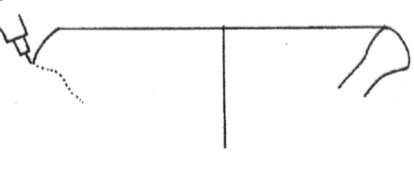

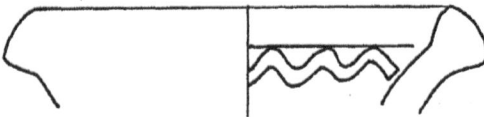

The basic outline, profile and cross-section of the vessel rim are now reconstructed.

Next, measure carefully and draw in any decorations. Any notable ridges or grooves are indicated with a horizontal line. All decorations including incising or painting on the inside of the vessel are on the right side of the center line. (North American method)

None of these interior decoration lines touch the inside line of the cross-section, but stop short of it by 1-2 mm. This is an illustration norm which is maintained when the drawing is inked for publication.

Any decorations or ridges on the outside of the vessel are measured and drawn to the left of the center line.

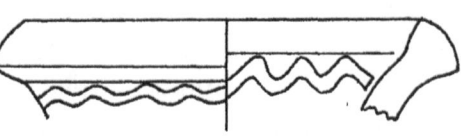

Unlike the interior decorations, these lines and decorations **do** touch the outline of the sherd.

Little dashes continuing the profile and cross-section further down the page, simply indicate that the actual vessel does not end where the illustration does. However, it is unknown exactly how far down it continues.

When the illustration is inked for publication, do not ink directly over the pencil drawing!

Place a sheet of mylar over the pencil drawing and trace with a rapidograph or fountain pen onto the mylar. Or use a WACOM tablet.

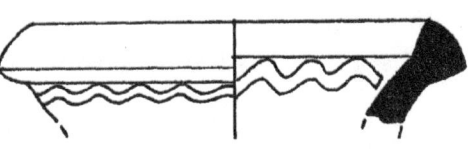

The cross section on the right is inked in solid black. The decorations are sometimes filled in with stipples to indicate a medium color like red or grey.

The pencil drawings can be kept as back up if the inked work is misplaced.

Always photograph, photocopy, and scan all pencil and inked work. This is also in case the pencil or inked work is misplaced. This happens more often than you might expect.

An added benefit is that the copied work can be placed into the artist's portfolio.

Always number, label, date and sign all the pencil and inked illustrations, and keep a running list of your work. This list could be handwritten. However, an excel or other data base would be much better. Keep this in multiple locations in case a copy becomes lost or erased.

CERAMICS/POTTERY

b) Bases

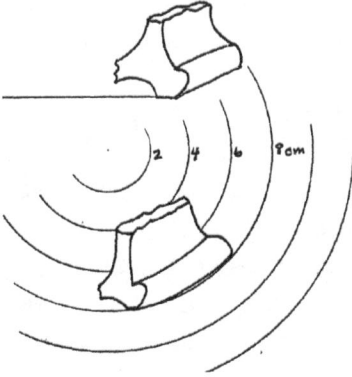

Bases are drawn much the same as rims. When drawing bases, the horizontal line is drawn near the bottom of the page, and vertical centre line is drawn up from it instead of down from it.

Determine the stance of the base sherd by placing the sherd right side up, on a flat surface and checking if any light passes under the base edge. (see rim sherd drawing)

Next, determine the diameter of the base by placing the base in its correct stance on a diameter ring chart. Choose the diameter line that best matches the outside edge of the base.

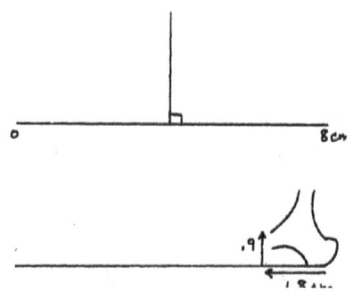

Next, draw a horizontal line at the bottom of a piece of paper. Mark the center of this line and draw a vertical line up from that center line.

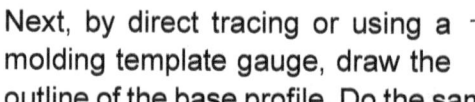

To determine where to place the outline of the base, hold the base in its correct stance and measure

across and up as you did with the rim sherd. Then transfer those measurements to the paper.

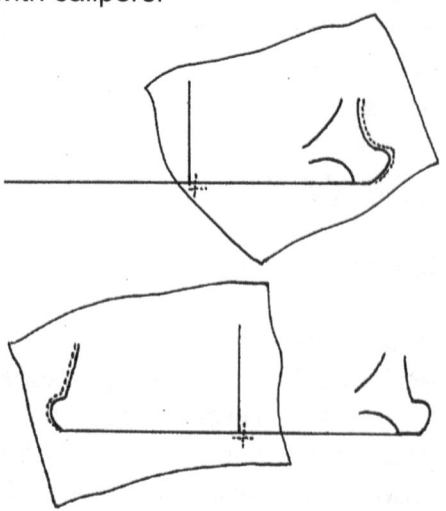

Next, by direct tracing or using a molding template gauge, draw the outline of the base profile. Do the same for the interior. Double check measurements and thicknesses with calipers.

Once the profile of the base is drawn, the exterior side is drawn with the help of tracing paper, just as when drawing rim sherds.

Place the tracing paper over the profile drawing and both vertical and horizontal base lines. Mark the intersection of the two baselines with a cross or x, and trace only the exterior side of the profile.

Flip the tracing paper over, face down on the left side of the drawing. Line up the cross or x on the intersection of the two baselines. Then line up the traced exterior outline with the horizontal baseline on the left. Trace over this outline pressing hard so some of the lead on the backside will rub off on the paper beneath. Remove the tracing paper and darken up the outline on the left side.

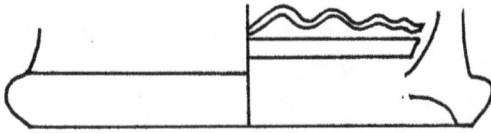 Draw in the decorations and ridge lines on the inside and outside of the vessel, in the same way as you would for a rim sherd. Notice that decoration lines on the inside of the vessel do not touch the profile on the right side of the drawing.

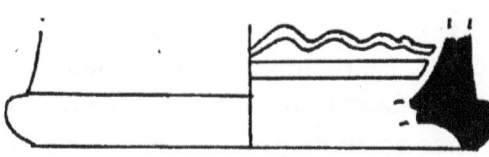 When inking, do not ink directly over the pencil drawings. Place a sheet of velum over the pencil drawing and ink by tracing with a rapiograph pen or use the WACOM tablet.

The profile cross section is filled in with solid black. Small dashes on either end of the broken profile indicates that the pot continued at one time, before it was broken.

CERAMICS/POTTERY

c) Body Sherds

Body sherds do not have as much information which can be retrieved as do rim or base sherds. Therefore, they are usually easier to draw.

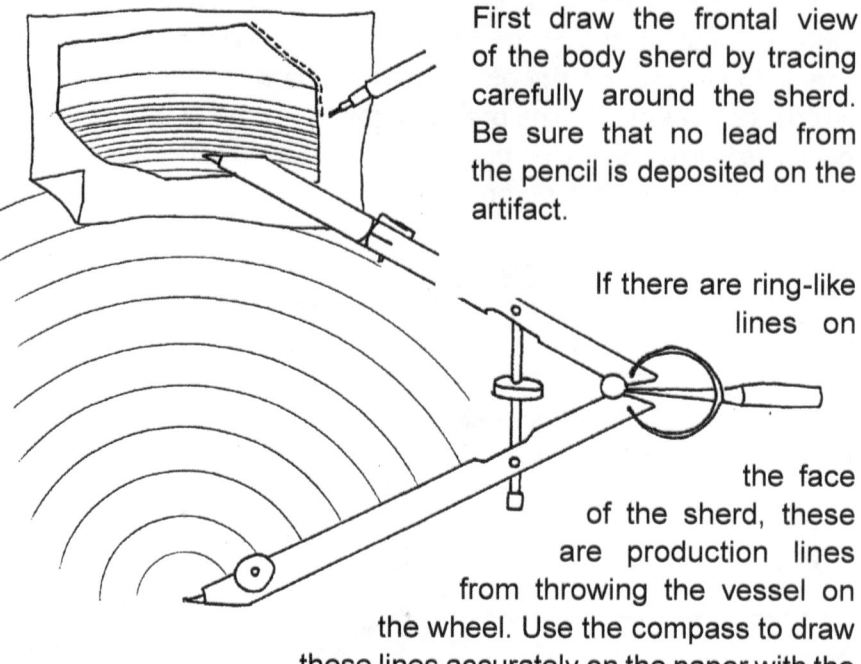

First draw the frontal view of the body sherd by tracing carefully around the sherd. Be sure that no lead from the pencil is deposited on the artifact.

If there are ring-like lines on the face of the sherd, these are production lines from throwing the vessel on the wheel. Use the compass to draw these lines accurately on the paper with the correct diameter. The diameter ring chart can help with this. Line up the actual lines with the ring chart lines.

Draw the profile, or cross section of the sherd to the right of this frontal view.

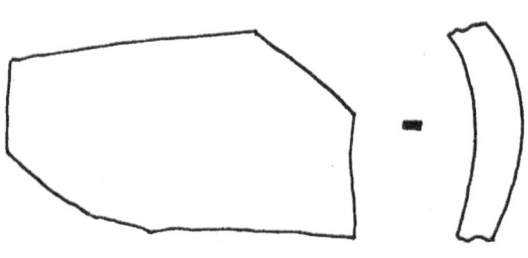

When drawing the profile of the body sherd, always double check the thicknesses of the sherd with calipers. If the stance can be ascertained, even without a rim or base, the draw the profile at this correct stance.
(see next page for tips)

The diameter and stance of a body sherd can sometimes be determined, although it is difficult. Here are some tips:

Wheel production lines are almost always found on wheel-made pottery. These lines were created by the craftsperson producing the vessel. The lines were made by holding the hand or other implement against the wet clay of the vessel while it was turning on the wheel. The result is usually lines of varying depth and width which are somewhat horizontal. This can help us to estimated the stance of the vessel.

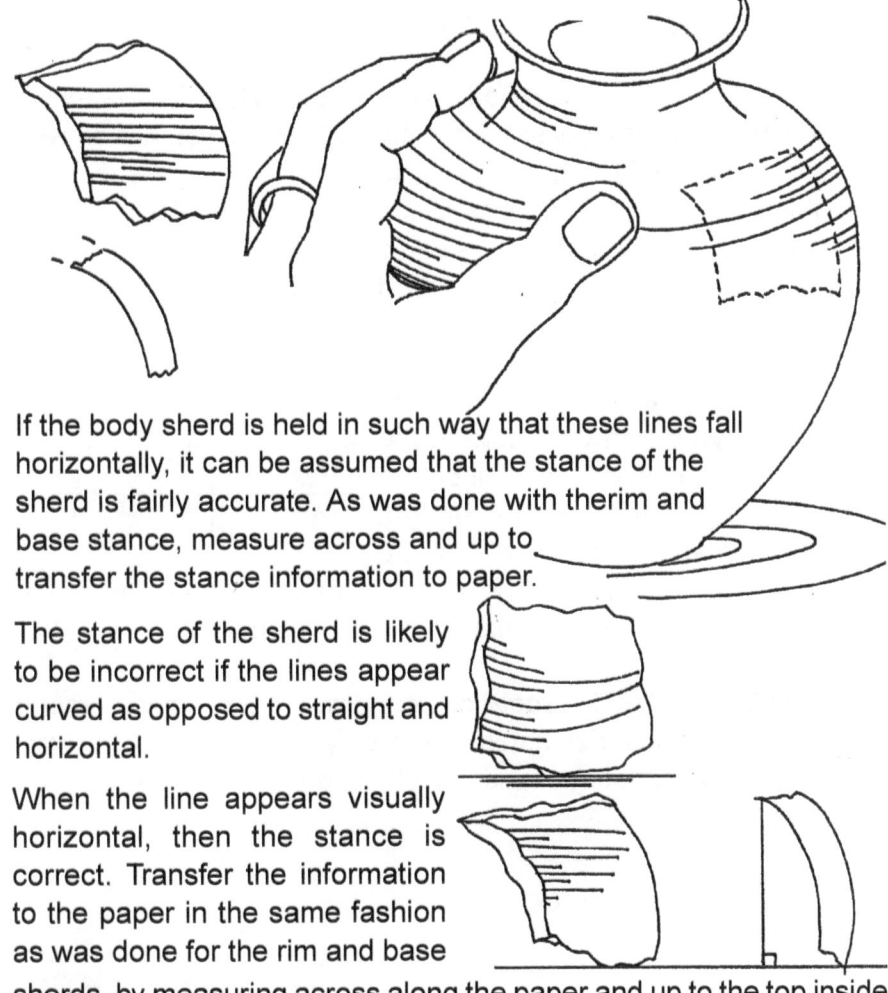

If the body sherd is held in such way that these lines fall horizontally, it can be assumed that the stance of the sherd is fairly accurate. As was done with therim and base stance, measure across and up to transfer the stance information to paper.

The stance of the sherd is likely to be incorrect if the lines appear curved as opposed to straight and horizontal.

When the line appears visually horizontal, then the stance is correct. Transfer the information to the paper in the same fashion as was done for the rim and base sherds, by measuring across along the paper and up to the top inside edge of the sherd.

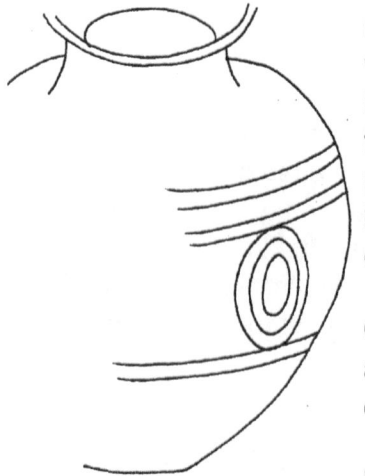

Sometimes the artisan who created the vessel would paint linear decoration on it as it turned on the wheel. As a result, the lines are horizontal. Similarly with the production lines, these decorations can help the artifact illustrator determine the original stance of the vessel.

Circular decorations can be measured and drawn on the illustration with a compass.

Body sherds naturally become thicker towards the base of a vessel. So, if the body sherd you are drawing goes from thin to thicker, it is possible that this piece came from close to the base on the original vessel. This could help you decide which end of the sherd was oriented in an upwards position.

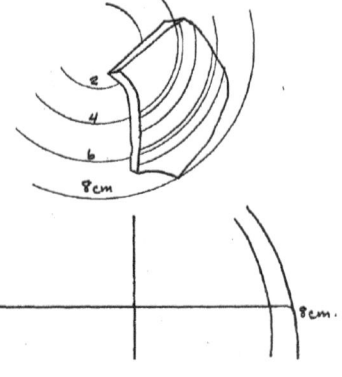

The diameter of a body sherd can be estimated by holding the sherd in the correct stance position. Place it on the diameter ring chart and look straight down on the sherd and chart. Line up the curves of the chart with those of the artifact to find an estimated diameter. Transfer that information to your illustration.

NOTE: It is important to record on your drawing any measurements which are estimates. Estimates should only occur due to badly worn or broken sherds, not because of lack of care by the illustrator.

CERAMICS/POTTERY

d) Entire and Partial Vessels

Drawing entire vessels requires many of the techniques already outlined in the previous sections because all entire vessels and partial vessel possess some, or all the following: a rim, base and body. However, a few other skills are also needed to bring all these parts together to create a whole vessel.

Although it may seem that the simplest method of drawing an entire vessel is to take a photograph of it with a black-and-white scale, and then draw it from the photo. However, there are many reasons why this method does not work. It is not accurate as the camera lens and angle of the camera may cause distortion. Also, the cross-section will have to be added by additional measurements of the actual vessel. It is much easier and more accurate to draw everything directly from the vessel itself.

A valuable tool for drawing entire vessels consists of three rulers or meter sticks set up in the same arrangement as illustrated below. The vertical ruler and the lowermost horizontal ruler must be set at exactly 90 degrees to each other. The third ruler is horizontal as well. It is attached at right angles to the vertical ruler with an adjustable but rigid bracket. The bracket is held to the vertical ruler by a screw and elastic band. The bracket allows the illustrator the freedom to move the horizontal ruler in and out as needed. A line level on the base and on the horizontal ruler are very important.

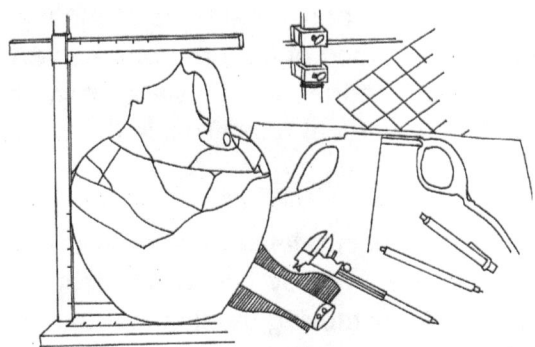

If possible, measure the diameter of the base and the mouth (rim) of the pot on the diameter ring chart or with calipers. Keep a record of these numbers.

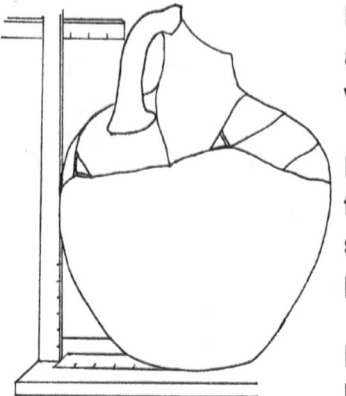

Place the vessel on the bottom platform, as close to the vertical ruler as possible, with the vessel touching the vertical ruler.

Next, prepare your paper. Place see through vellum on a piece of graph paper so you can see the grid lines through the paper.

Draft an x/y scale on your paper. One line horizontal, near the bottom of your paper, and the second line at 90 degrees to the first along the left-hand vertical edge of your paper. Mark in the points for each centimeter along both lines. These lines will represent the lower horizontal and vertical rulers.

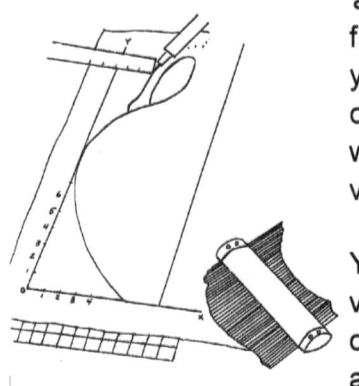

You will be drawing only one side of the vessel at a time. The side and profile closest to the vertical ruler is the one you are drawing.

Next, plot the diameter of the base of the vessel and the distance of the base from the vertical ruler. Then measure the height of the vessel by using the upper horizontal ruler. Mark this point on your paper. Then plot the distance of the rim from the vertical ruler, and the width of the mouth of the vessel. Mark on your paper where the vessel touches the vertical ruler. This is the widest point of the vessel.

There are two ways to accurately measure in the exact profile of the vessel. This can be done by taking numerous horizontal and vertical measurements by moving the floating ruler and transfer the measurements to the paper. Then draw the profile by joining the dots. The second method is by measuring the profile in sections with the molding profile gauge. Remember to hold the lines of the gauge perfectly horizontal to acquire an accurate profile. Then trace the gauge silhouette onto the paper one section at a time.

It is very rare that a vessel is perfectly symmetrical. However, if it is, the opposite side of the vessel can be drawn by using the tracing technique we used with rims and bases.

Often, a vessel is asymmetrical. This may be due to its sagging before firing. In such a case, to draw the second side of the vessel accurately, simply turn the vessel 180 degrees and measure and draw in the same fashion as with the first side. You can check sections of this profile with the molding profile gauge.

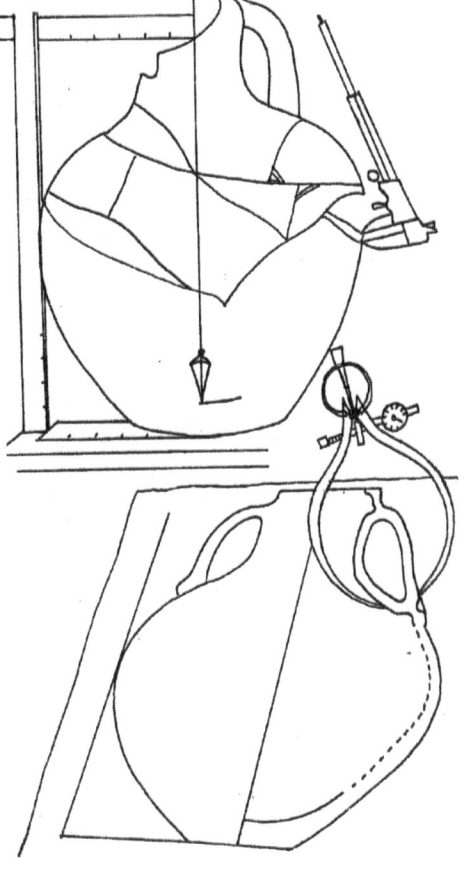

Double check that the diameters of the rim, base, neck, shoulder, and widest point of the vessel are correct.

Next, check where you can determine the thickness of the sides of the vessel.

These measurements are difficult to acquire especially if the mouth of the vessel is narrow. If the sides of the vessel are incomplete, then measurements can be taken through the side of the vessel. Also, special bow calipers with clock gauges on the handle can be used as far as the arms can reach, and not further.

To measure the thickness of the base is a bit simpler. You can hang either a long ruler or a plumb bob inside the vessel. With a horizontal ruler, mark the vertical ruler or string and transfer that information to your drawing.

Finally, draw in the decorations and ridges on the interior and exterior using the same method as we used for rim, base, and body sherds.

CHAPTER 3
Lithics

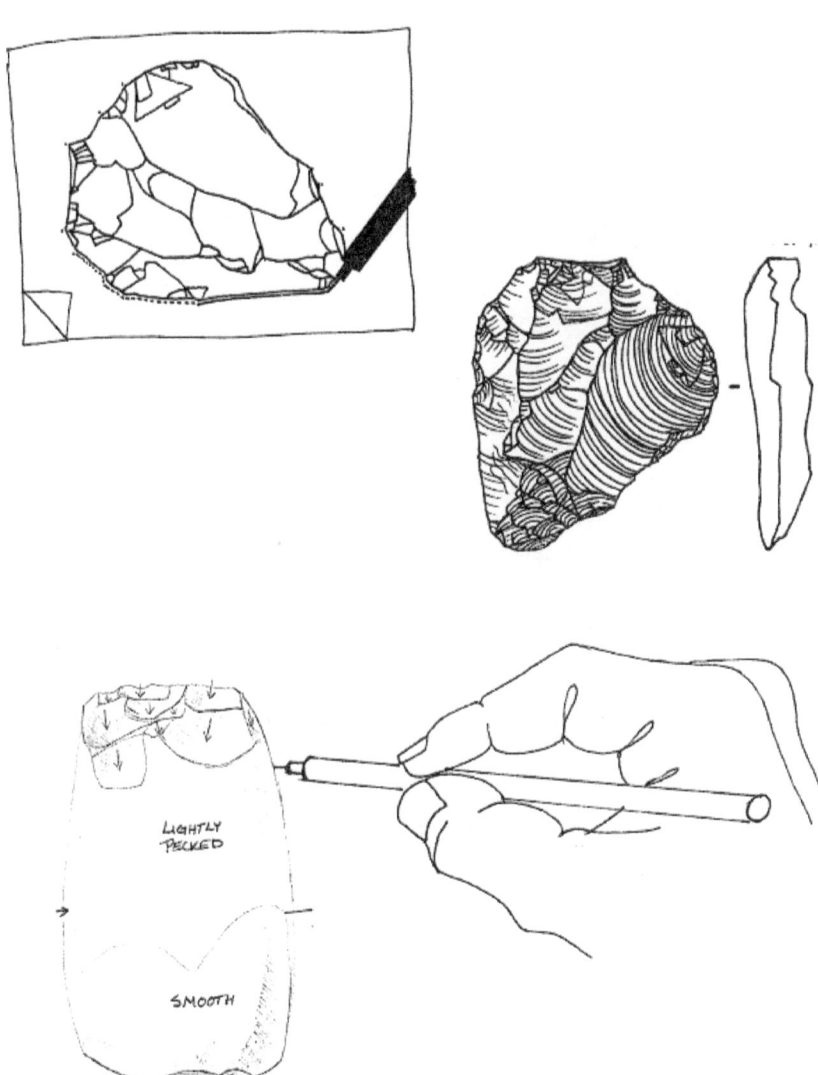

CHAPTER 3

Lithics

The name lithics refers to those artifacts made from stone. There are a wide variety of lithic artifacts, such as axes, adzes, arrow points, spear points, knives, scrapers, blades, sickle blades, threshing sledge blades, burins, drills, grinders, mortar and pestle, stone bowls and net sinkers. Stone artifacts are very widespread around the world, and date back to the beginning of human existence. Every archaeological illustrator will be asked at one time or another to illustrate lithic objects.

A good illustration provides a much greater wealth of information than a photograph would. It informs the viewer of the material from which the artifact was made, how it was made, what the function of the artifact was, and the use wear patterns on it. Because of this, it is invaluable for an illustrator to work closely with a lithic archaeologist to understand lithic technology. When an illustrator understands the material's inherent properties as well as the technological practices of the people who produced the artifact, more accurate illustrations result. An in depth understanding of the material can be attained by attempting to reproduce an artifact with scrap materials. Again, working with a lithics expert is invaluable when learning how to reproduce lithic artifacts and thereby create more accurate illustrations.

Illustrators can also build up their knowledge of illustration conventions by reading all the books available on the subject. Illustrating stone artifacts requires more of an artistic eye than ceramic illustrating does. The uniqueness of each lithic artifact means that the illustrations must be more three-dimensional looking. This is achieved by creating darker and lighter areas on the drawing. The two conventions for shading are as follows. With the ground stone, such as the axes, adzes, net sinkers and stone bowls, the shading in ink is created using the stippling technique. This consists of hundreds of small dots. The closer the dots, the darker the shadow. The chipped stone artifacts are drawn almost entirely with line, either solid or dashed, with some stippling. Both techniques produce three-dimensional looking illustrations.

Stone artifacts are always drawn with a light source from the top left.

As a result, the deepest shadow on the artifact is at the bottom right. The best way to train your eye and draw a lithic artifact accurately, is to place the object in a very strong, raking light, originating from the top left. Natural light is the best. This will emphasize the dark and light separation.

The ability to draw lithics is a skill acquired through patience and lots of practice. Start with the easiest pieces first, such as single flakes, to warm up and build up your skills.

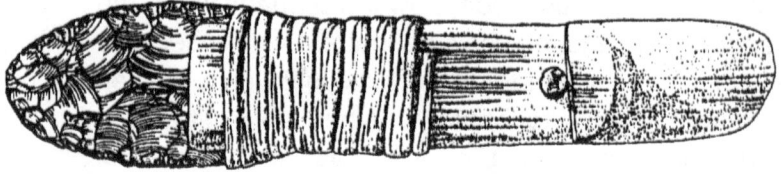

LITHICS

a) chipped stone: technology summary

In the past, creating chipped stone artifacts always followed a prescribed order. The material, such as chert or obsidian would be found in nodule form in an embankment and surrounded or encapsulated in other material such as limestone. The chert or obsidian would be worked out of the matrix. These nodules were often found far from the technician's home base. Therefore, on the spot, the nodule would be worked down to a usable core by taking off the undesirable materials such as the cortex and poor-quality chert with fractures. Thus, the technician cut down on the weight of the core which needed to be carried home. This also prevented the production of poor-quality flakes later at the home base. The primary trimming into usable flakes, smaller blanks or cores was often done at the gathering site as well, making transport even easier. Usually, back at the home base, the actual flaking and tool production began.

Removal of flakes from the core was done by percussion flaking. The implement used was either a hammerstone, metal hammer (in modern times) or similar tool; one that could exert a moderate amount of force. Initially, when lithic production first appeared in ancient sites, the flakes were short and wide, mostly because the cores were not set up properly. It was eventually discovered that if the core was prepared properly, with long sides and a flat top platform, the resulting flakes did not have to be short and wide. Proper shaping of the core allowed for the production of long flakes or blades, which were twice as long as they were wide. This technological change in production occurred in the Neolithic Period c. 7000BC.

When a core is struck, waves radiate into the core from the point of impact, much like the ripples in a pond when a stone is thrown in. The more a core is struck, the weaker it becomes, as fractures appear in the material caused by the waves. Good lithic technicians do not strike a core more than is necessary, and they make sure that each blow produces a flake.

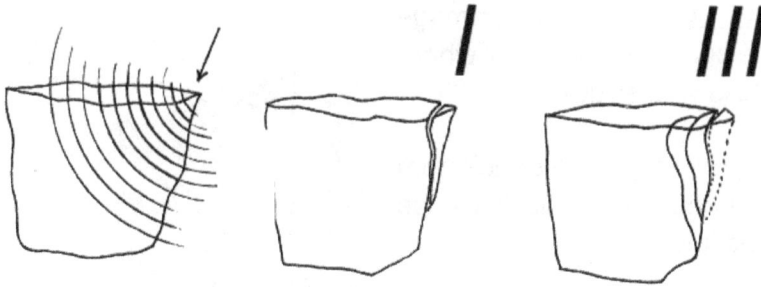

LITHICS

b) Lithics Terminology

CORE: A large piece of stone material such as chert or obsidian from which flakes are struck.

CORTEX: The exterior surface of the core which is usually weathered and rough.

FLAKE: The piece of the core or the lithic which has been struck off. A flake has a platform where the striking tool hit the core. It also has a bulb of procession, undulating waves of production, ventral and dorsal faces, and is usually less than twice as long as it is wide, unless it is a long blade. When working on a lithic tool, the strike on the top side of the tool, will usually cause a flake to break off from the opposite face or bottom of the tool.

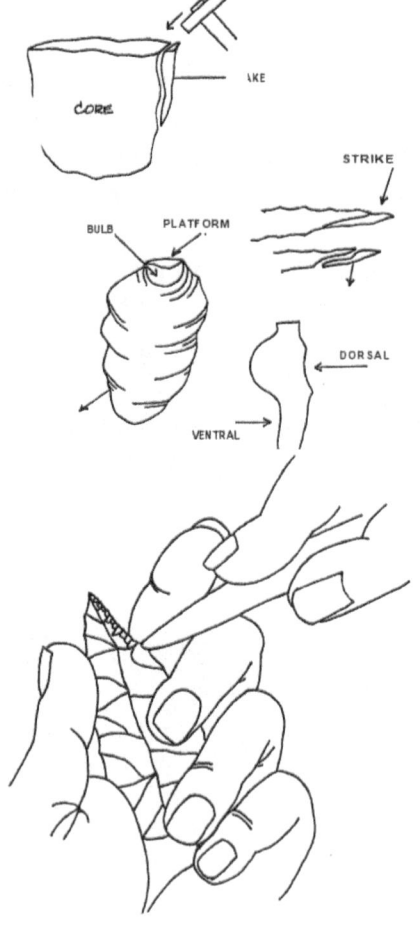

FLAKE SCAR: The mirror image on the core or worked tool where the flake was struck off.

BLADE: A long flake struck from a prepared core. It is twice as long as it is wide.

PERCUSSION FLAKING: Large primary flakes taken off the core with a large tool such as a hammerstone, which can exert much force. The flakes that come off are usually large and rough, with a large bulb.

<u>PRESSURE FLAKING</u>: Fine edge flaking in the final stages of tool production is used to fine tune the shape the lithic tool and sharpen the edges. This method is achieved by using a small tool such as an antler tine. The lithic is held on a pad on the thigh, and the tine is pressed down on the edge of the lithic until a flake pops off the opposing side. These flakes are small to medium size.

<u>RETOUCH FLAKING</u>: Can occur spontaneously when the lithic tool is being used (such as a scraper used to clean a hide), or intentionally to sharpen the edges of the tool. This can be achieved by pressure flaking or by pressing the edge of the tool on an angle on a hard stone so that the small flakes pop off. These flakes are very small.

<u>THE STRIKING PLATFORM</u>: Is where the hammerstone strikes the core. A flake of chert or obsidian is sheared off the core due to the force of the blow. The platform of the flake is on the proximal end of the flake

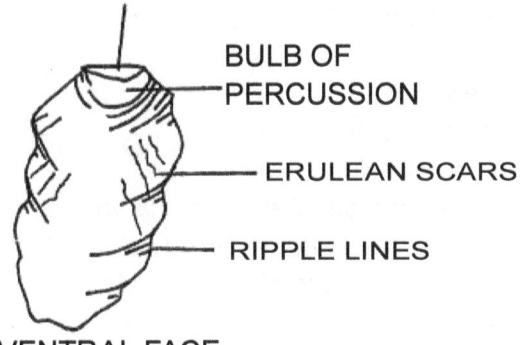

STRIKING PLATFORM

BULB OF PERCUSSION

ERULEAN SCARS

RIPPLE LINES

VENTRAL FACE

<u>BULB OF PERCUSSION</u>: The protruding, rounded area just below the platform on the proximal end of the ventral side of the flake is called the bulb of percussion. Larger bulbs are usually associated with blows of greater force.

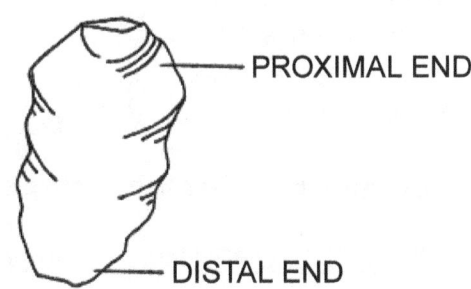

PROXIMAL END

DISTAL END

<u>THE PROXIMAL END</u>: The striking platform is on the proximal end of the flake. If an illustration is drawn with the production of the flake in mind, then the illustration will have the proximal end up as seen to the right.

DISTAL END: The thin, feathered out area of the flake is called the distal end of the flake

VENTRAL FACE: The side of the flake which was facing into the core before it was struck is the ventral face. On this face we find the bulb of percussion, erulian scars, ripple lines, and hinge and step fractures. These are all drawn in with lines. Both the flake struck off and the scar on the core have the exact same characteristics but in mirror image to each other.

DORSAL FACE: The side of the flake which was facing out from the core when the flake was struck, is call

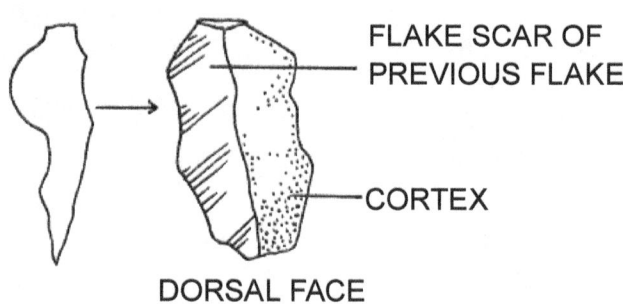

FLAKE SCAR OF PREVIOUS FLAKE

CORTEX

DORSAL FACE

the dorsal face. Visible on this face are the scars of the flakes which were previously taken off, and sometimes some of the cortex of the core is also found here. When drawn and inked, the cortex is stippled.

FLAKE SCARS: The marks left on a lithic artifact after a flake has been struck off.

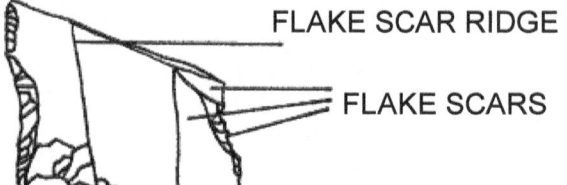

FLAKE SCAR RIDGE

FLAKE SCARS

SCAR RIDGES: The raised edges separating the flake scars.

HINGE FRACTURE: Usually hinge fractures occur if a metal hammer is used to produce the flakes. The flake rips off the core with such force, that the end of the flake does not feather at the dorsal end but snaps off like a small step. This can also occur due to an anomaly in the core fabric.

ERULEAN SCARS: Short, wiggly lines which radiate out from the bulb of percussion like the rays of the sun. These are helpful in identifying the strike direction.

RUNNERS OR LADDERS: The step-like scars at the edges of the flake scars.

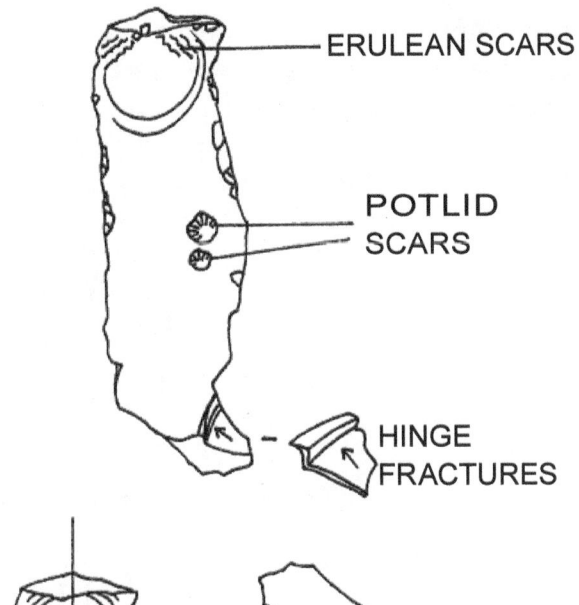

ERULEAN SCARS

POTLID SCARS

HINGE FRACTURES

POTLID SCARS: Circular-shaped flakes which pop off a chert or obsidian artifact due to heating. The lithic artifact may have been put in a fire.

ORIENTATION: The way in which the artifact illustration is set up on the paper. It depends on the choice of the person asking for the illustrations.

PRODUCTION ORIENTATION: This orientation focusses on how the flake was produced. The

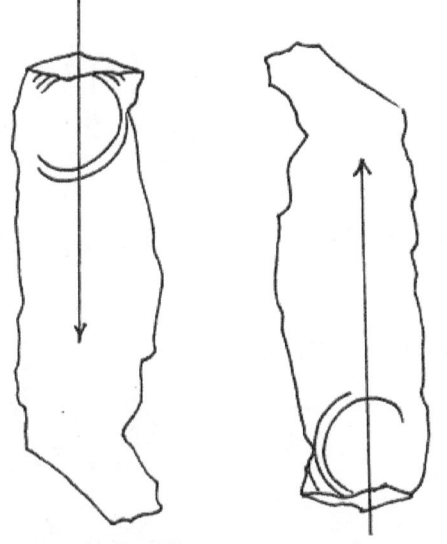

PRODUCTION ORIENTATION

AESTHETIC ORIENTATION

flake was struck from the top where the bulb is. So, the flake is drawn with the bulb at the top of the page.

<u>AESTHETIC ORIENTATION:</u> In this orientation, the heavier part of the flake, or bulb, is at the bottom of the page.

<u>ORIENTATION:</u> Illustrations are often done in different ways based on which countries the directors of the projects are from. Generally, North American Archaeologists will orient their drawings one way and the Europeans will orient their drawings in another way. This applies not only to lithic illustrations, but pottery and 3D illustrations as well. Below the two opposing methodologies are illustrated. Check with your director to see which they would prefer.

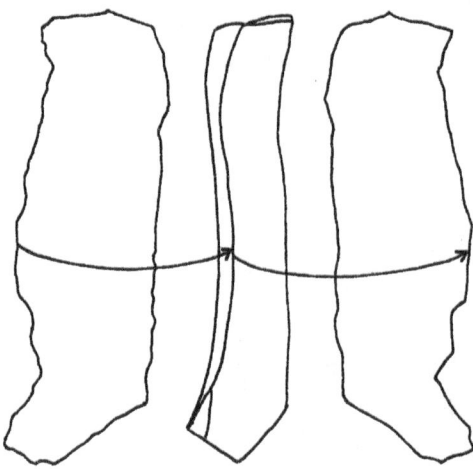

<u>AMERICAN ORIENTATION</u>: dorsal face, left distal profile, ventral face

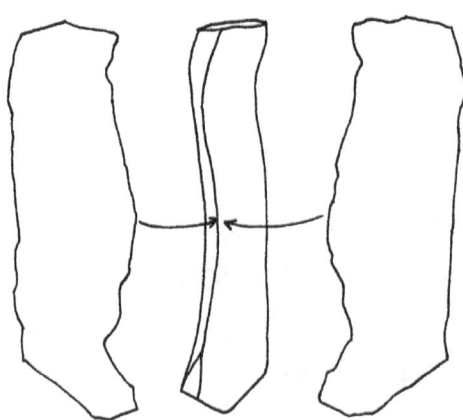

<u>EUROPEAN ORIENTATION</u>: ventral face, right interior profile, dorsal face

LITHICS

c) drawing chipped stone artifacts

Chipped stone is perhaps the most difficult of all the artifacts to draw. This is because of the many facets of the chert, obsidian, flint or greywhackie, as well as the three-dimensionality of the artifact. Therefore, the thicker objects are drawn much like a 3D object. Flatter, thinner objects such as flakes, scrapers and points are a bit simpler to draw.

Begin by choosing the face (side) of the artifact which best demonstrates the characteristics which you wish to illustrate. This is usually the dorsal side of a blade, scraper, or other tool, or the most carefully worked face of a projectile point.

For paper, I use a sheet of see-through vellum with graph paper under it. This makes the drawing much clearer than if you draw directly on the graph paper. The graph paper under the velum helps you to line up the different views of the artifact.

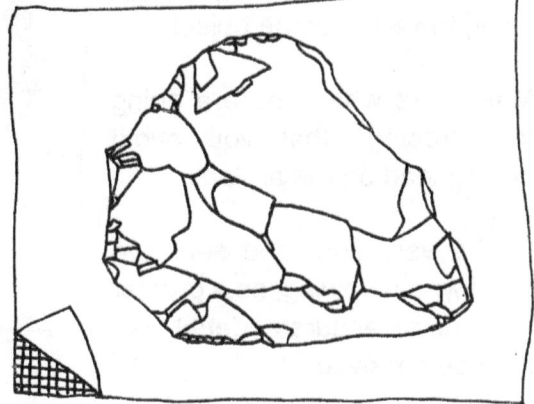

Place the artifact flat on the drawing paper. It can be held in place with a kneadable eraser. Just make sure that the eraser does not leave any mark or residue on the artifact.

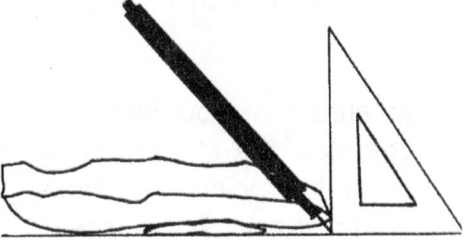

Plasticine would not work because it would leave a greasy mark on the object.

Using the set square or plastic triangle, trace the silhouette of the artifact on the paper. Hold the triangle at 90 degrees to the edge of the object and with a pencil, mark all the major points around the perimeter of the object on the paper. Now you have the object's main points drawn on the paper.

Double check the accuracy of the locations of the major points by closing one eye and looking straight down along the edge of the artifact.

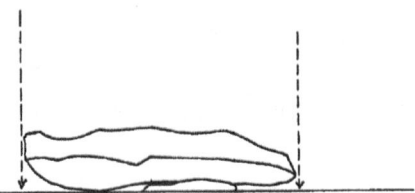

The main points you marked previously with the plastic triangle you can now join with an outline of the artifact looking straight down along the edge of the object.

Make sure when you are doing this' tracing', that you avoid putting lead on the artifact.

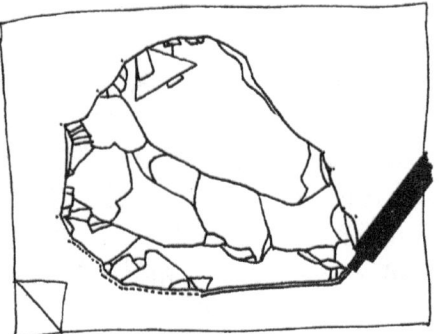

Use a very light and sensitive hand when drawing, as a greater amount of accurate detail can then be retrieved.

And any errors can be erased easily.

Make sure that you have not exaggerated the sharpness or depth of the points and flake scars when tracing the outline of the artifact.

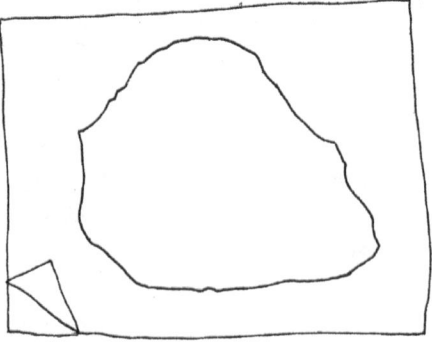

Be precise. The outline of the artifact depicts the character of the artifact. This means it provides us with information such as the technique used to make the object, what it was used for, and any changes that occurred to the object during and after use.

Now remove the artifact from the paper and darken the outline. Again, do this carefully, so as not to add information that doesn't exist in the artifact.

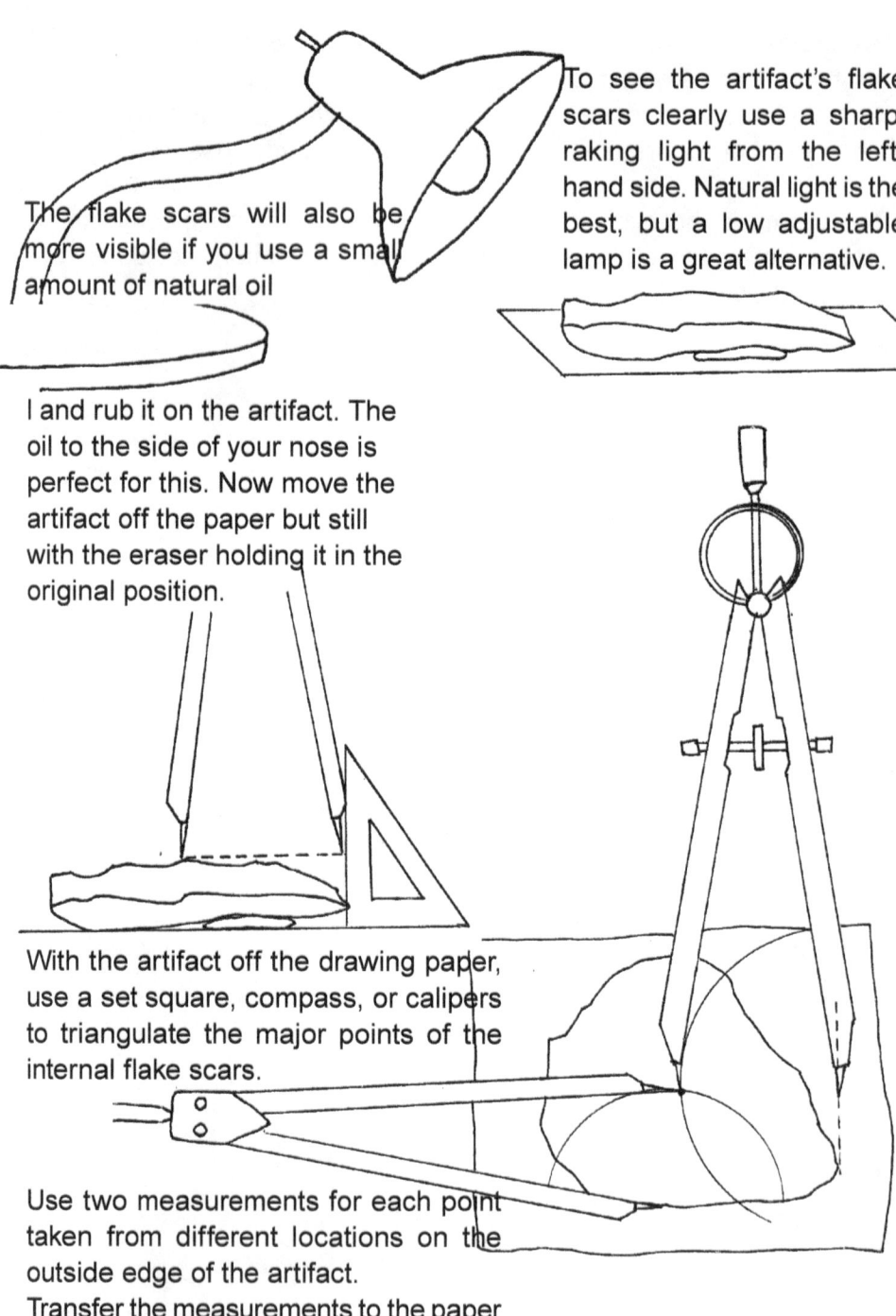

To see the artifact's flake scars clearly use a sharp, raking light from the left-hand side. Natural light is the best, but a low adjustable lamp is a great alternative.

The flake scars will also be more visible if you use a small amount of natural oil

I and rub it on the artifact. The oil to the side of your nose is perfect for this. Now move the artifact off the paper but still with the eraser holding it in the original position.

With the artifact off the drawing paper, use a set square, compass, or calipers to triangulate the major points of the internal flake scars.

Use two measurements for each point taken from different locations on the outside edge of the artifact.

Transfer the measurements to the paper with the artifact outline on it.

Draw arcs on the paper equal to the two measurements. Where the two arcs meet, draw a point. Continue doing this for all the major points on this face of the object. Then by closely observing the characteristics of the flake scars, join the dots.

Calipers are another tool you could use but, in this case, will need special awareness. Using calipers could give you a distortion especially if the artifact is thick and sits high from the table surface.

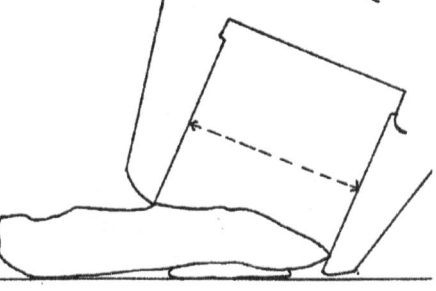

The challenge is to make sure that the calipers are perfectly horizontal not on a diagonal angle as in this diagram. This measurement is too long

A ruler with a line level on it could help to see where horizontal is. Then place the calipers in this position and measure. Transfer that measurement to the paper. Again, use triangulation and measure into the point from two different points on the perimeter of the object.

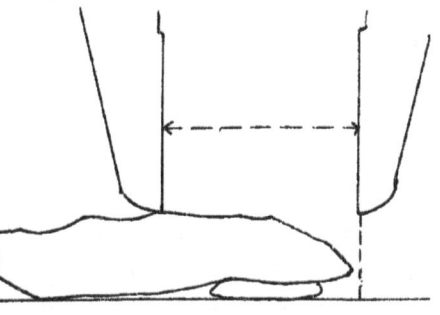

Continue using the same technique for all flake scars. Then join the dots by carefully drawing in all the flake scars.

You can double check all these points with a quick, one eye scan.

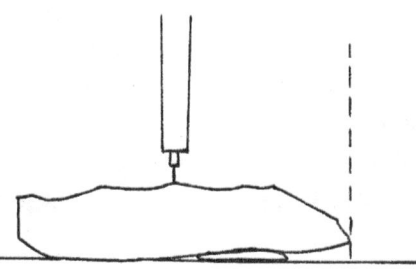

Place the object over the drawing, lining up the outlines.
Close one eye and look directly down onto the artifact.
Hold the pencil above one of the main points of the flake scars. Don't touch the artifact with the pencil.

Without moving the pencil or your eye, remove the artifact, bring the pencil straight down to the paper. Make a dot.

Now check to see if this dot matches the point previously measured with compasses, calipers and set squares. and drawn in. If it doesn't match, then remeasure again and correct.

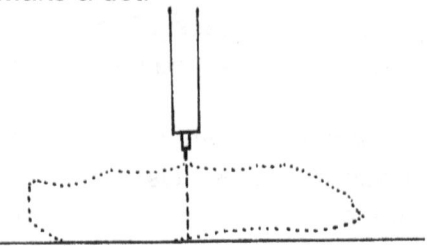

Fill in all the smaller flake scars using the same method as above. These smaller scars are no less important that the bigger scars just because they are small. Usually, these flake scars will help to identify the techniques used to create the artifact and with also show signs of use or retouch.

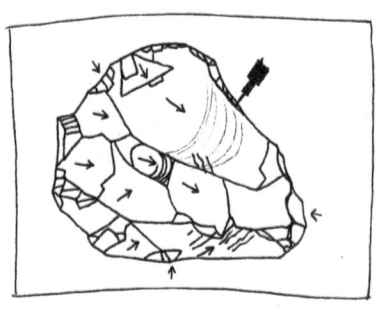

Now you will rotate the object in your hands in the raking light to see if you can identify the direction that the flakes were struck off the object during production. Platforms, bulbs of percussion, erulean scars, hinge fractures, step fractures, and the wavy concentric ripple scars can

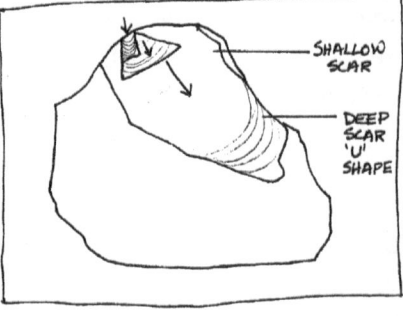

all help you identify the direction of the strike. Draw a small arrow down the center of each flake scar starting at the bulb end of the flake scar.

Next, draw in some of the wave or ripple scars to indicate the depth of the flake. A relatively flat row of concentric lines indicates a shallow flake scar. 'U-shaped' concentric lines denote a deeper flake scar.

At this point using the raking light from the top left, you can shade in some of the flake scars to show light and dark areas which you will recreate when inking the drawing.

Next, draw the profile of the artifact. The profile is very helpful in drawings. With the profile we can see if the artifact is thick or thin, curved or straight. It can also show valuable use wear information.

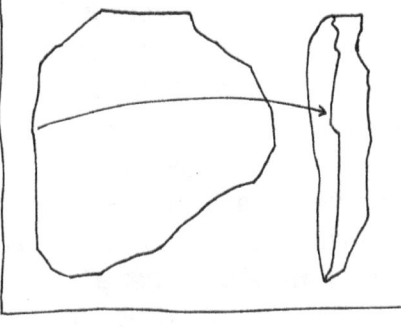

The orientation of the profile depends on which convention you have been asked to use, European or North American. Whichever one you use, stay consistent. Here, the North American orientation is used.

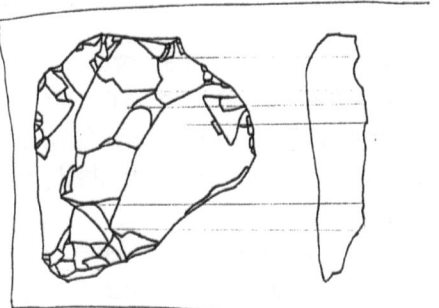

To avoid drawing the profile too long or short, and also to make sure that the outline is accurate, lightly draw horizontal projection lines from the major points on the dorsal drawing over to the profile drawing.

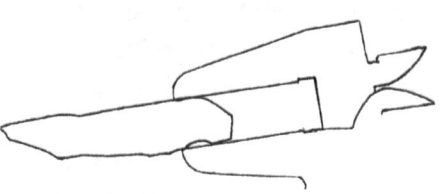

Because your paper is see-through and on top of graph paper it should be easy to make sure all the lines are horizontal.

Within these projected lines, line up the object on its edge, and using the one-eye method, mark the major points on the outline, and fill in the outline

To avoid drawing the profile too thin or too thick, double check the thickness of the object with calipers.

If the archaeologist is only interested in showing the thickness of the object, the profile is then often shaded in black and inked solidly black. Sometimes the median line of the profile is the only thing required. Other times you will be requested to draw all the flake scars along the dorsal and ventral sides. In the latter case great care must be taken to make sure that all the flake scars drawn on the profile, line up with those on the dorsal and ventral views.

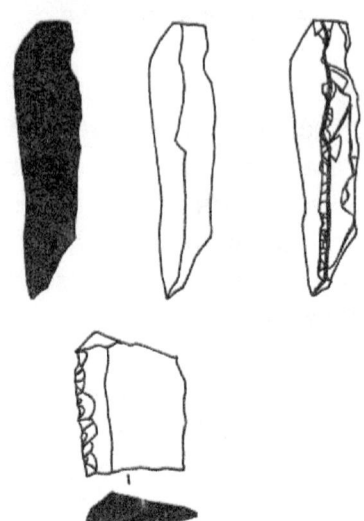

Cross-sections are often drawn below the dorsal side of blades or

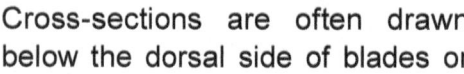

scrapers. This is to show how the blade or scraper was backed or dulled so it could be handled more easily by the user.

Finally, draw the ventral face of the artifact. The outline is easy. Trace the dorsal outline using tracing paper and a soft leaded pencil. Flip the tracing paper over, line it up in the correct location using the horizontal projections lines, and retrace, pressing relatively hard with the pencil. The lead on the underside will come off onto the vellum drawing paper. Remove the tracing paper and darken up the outline with H or 2H pencil.

Now draw in any flake scars using the same measuring method as above. Usually, the ventral side of the artifact will have less flake scars to draw. Make sure the flake scars line up with those on the profile. Draw in the direction arrows, wave or ripple lines and add the shading.

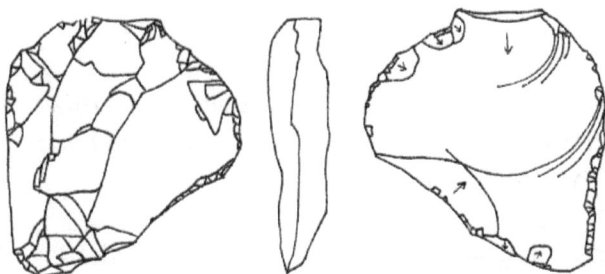

LITHICS

d) Inking

When inking the lithic illustration, do not ink over the pencil drawing. Use a good quality vellum or mylar which you place over the pencil drawing and then you ink on the mylar. The pencil drawing can be used as backup if the inked work is misplaced.

When inking, consideration must be given to how much an illustration will be reduced for publication. Make sure that you use thick enough pens otherwise beautifully delicate lines will disappear in the reduction. Also, if lines are too close together, they will form a black blob when reduced at the printers.

To shade in the flake scars, use concentric lines just like the ripple lines on the artifact itself. This is

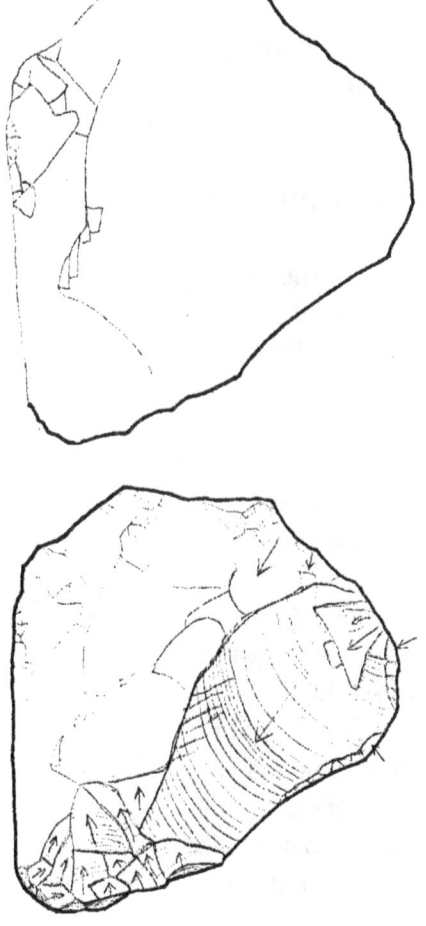

not totally realistic but is a clear and easily understood illustration convention.

Whether using a real or a tablet, outline the artifact with a #1 pen nib. Then with a slightly smaller nib, outline the flake scars and start drawing the concentric flake ripple scars.

Lines closer together create the concept of shadow. Lines further apart make that part of the flake look lighter. Lines can be broken to show a shine. Knowing that the light source is always from the upper left, this means there will be more shadow on the lower right and more lines. So, start shading here. Remember, less curved lines mean a shallow flake. More curved lines mean a deep flake.

When shading, one of the most important pieces of information to convey in the illustration is the direction of the blow that struck off the flake. The curved lines move away from the bulb of percussion and out following the direction of the blow. They also become less deep further away from the bulb.

As mentioned above, the depth of the flake scar is depicted by the curve of the lines. The more curved the lines, the deeper the flake.

The closer the lines are together, the darker the shadow. Do not make the drawing too dark or detail will be lost. Notice on the illustration to the right that

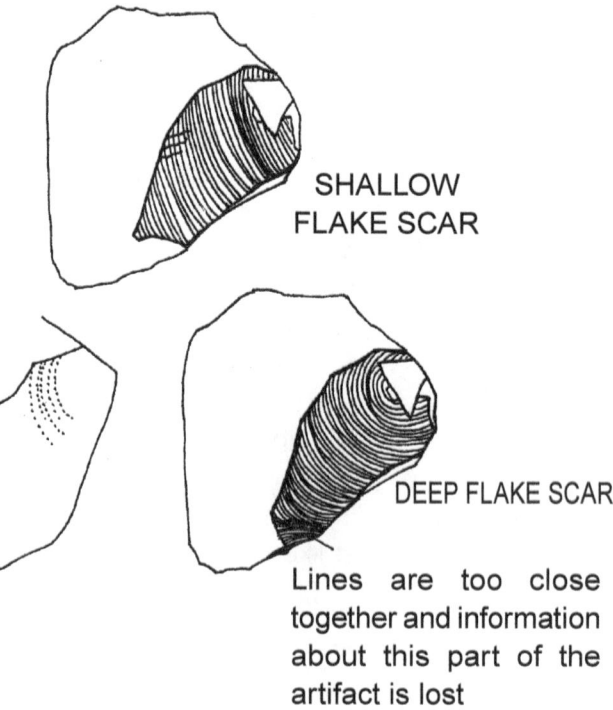

SHALLOW FLAKE SCAR

DEEP FLAKE SCAR

Lines are too close together and information about this part of the artifact is lost some of the ripple lines are too close together and create a black area. This will need to be redone. On mylar, the ink can be scraped away with a backed razor blade. Then the lines are inked in again and spaced properly apart.

If the object was made from granular material such as quartz, the ripple lines are inked in with broken lines

As you work from the lower right of the object towards the upper left, the shading becomes less. The lines will become fewer and further apart. The lines in the lighter part of the artifact also don't extend all the way from one side of the flake scar to the other side. This helps to give the impression of a shine from the light as well.

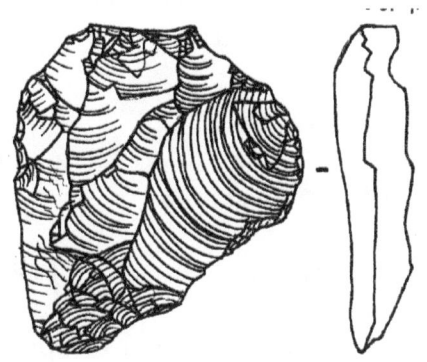

One technique which works well for publication is to enlarge the drawing to double its original size. This can be easily done with a photocopier and then inked with mylar over the photocopy. Ink it up with consideration that the inked illustration will be reduced so the lines need to be far enough apart to avoid blobbing. Make sure also that you use a thick enough ink line that the line doesn't disappear when the illustration is reduced

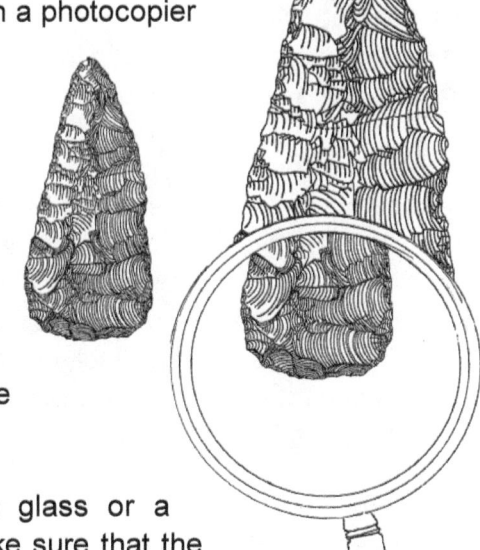

You can use a reduction glass or a reduction photocopy to make sure that the lines wont blob or disappear. Before publication, the inked illustration can be reduced to actual size with a PMT or photomechanical transfer. Also remember to put a simple scale of 5cm in the drawing which is enlarged in the inking so the exact size is achieved when published.

One advantage of this technique is that any small errors or blips in the inking will disappear if the original image is inked twice as large as the original and then reduced. This gives the illustration a more professional look.

LITHICS

e) groundstone

To be able to draw an artifact accurately, study how it is made. Ground stone artifacts are made by first creating the general shape with coarse pecking or chipping using a hammer stone. Next, the artifact is ground down with sand. In the case of the stone axe, the blade area is usually smoothed down the most to make it the sharpest part of the artifact. The distal end is duller.

The differences in pecking and grinding should be indicated on the pencil drawing with a line indicating the boundaries of the different facets. If the separation between the two types of pecking or chipping is gradual use a dotted line, or sharp, use a solid line.

As with the chipped stone, the ground stone pencil drawing is drawn three-dimensionally, with shading. The inked illustration is traced onto mylar from the pencil drawing and the shading is achieved through stippling as opposed to the solid lines used for chipped stone. Depending on the roughness or smoothness of the different facets of the ground stone artifact, the dots in the stippling can range from large and rough to small and precise. Any flake scar ripples are drawn with dotted lines.

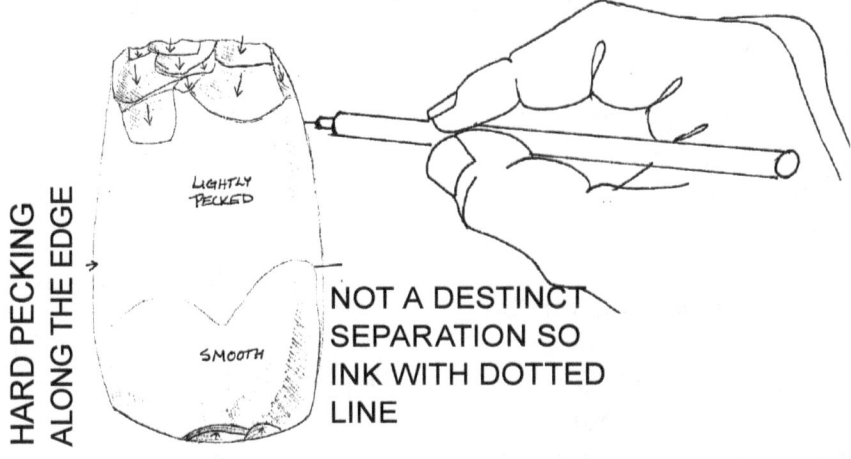

HARD PECKING ALONG THE EDGE

LIGHTLY PECKED

SMOOTH

NOT A DESTINCT SEPARATION SO INK WITH DOTTED LINE

Decide if you will draw the dorsal or ventral side of the artifact first. Then start by measuring and drawing the outline of the artifact on vellum using a set square and pencil.

Measure and draw in all the flake scars with set square and compass. Indicate the direction of the strike with an arrow, as you did with the chipped stone artifacts.

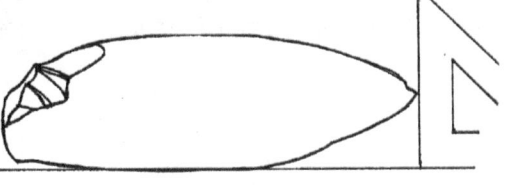

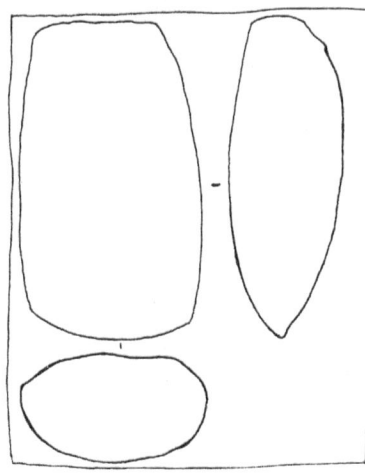

Now draw the profile, cross-section, and the opposing ventral side. If that side is totally smooth with no extra information, then it won't be important to draw the ventral side. Double check the widths, length, and thickness measurements with calipers.

Depending on what the archaeologist wants to emphasize, the profile and cross-section can either be totally black or with all the flake scars added in and measured accurately. See the chipped stone section.

When inking, outline the artifact with a #1 nib and work the inside with a nib one size smaller.

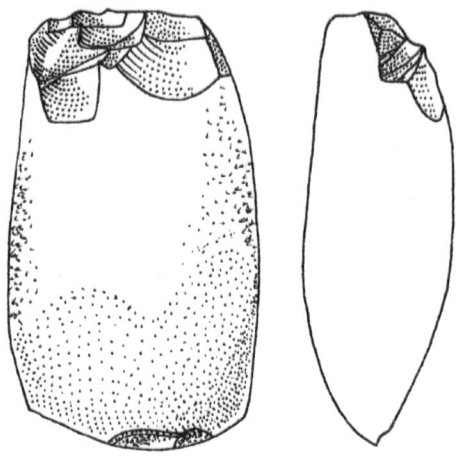

The heavy pecking on the stone surface is inked in coarse, fast stippling which is more like dashes than dots. The smooth sections are inked with small, precise stipples.

Any areas where the ground stone has been chipped like a chert artifact, these flake scars are inked with broken curved lines. The depth of the curvature of the line indicates the depth of the flake scar.

ABOUT THE AUTHOR

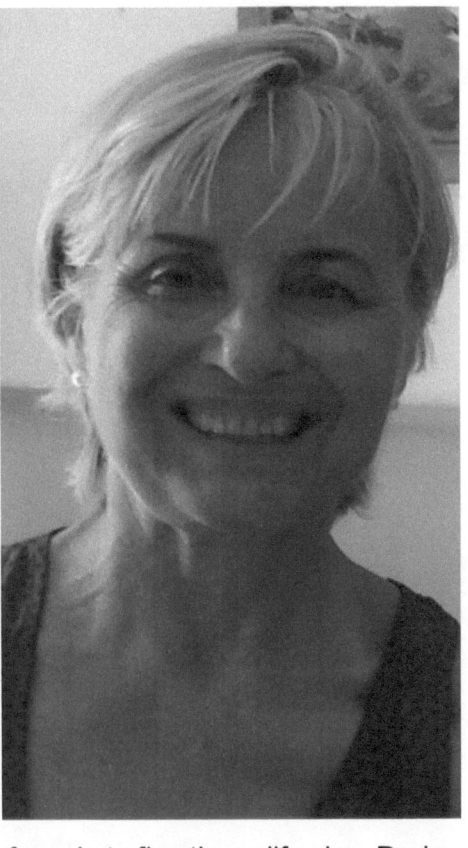

Janie Ravenhurst has illustrated artifacts on projects ranging from the Canadian Arctic to the Mediterranean shores of Cyprus. The sites she has worked on, both excavating and illustrating, range from 7,000 BCE to modern. This publication is a culmination of 45 years of archaeological illustration experience, as well as 60 years of drawing, painting and artistic creation since her earliest years and 35 years of teaching experience K-12. She has worked with numerous archaeologists in Canada and overseas whose projects have supplied her with the opportunity to draw thousands of artifacts including pottery, lithics and sculptures of various shapes and sizes from the size of a coin to five times life size. During field seasons, she has taught numerous undergrads how to draw artifacts, giving them yet another skill to add to their archaeological repertoire. She is excited to share her expertise with others through her Volume I: Illustration of Archaeological Artifacts.

www.ingramcontent.com/pod-product-compliance
Lightning Source LLC
Chambersburg PA
CBHW030745200526
45160CB00010B/39/J